The Positive Use of the Minister's Role

The Positive Use
of the
Minister's Role

by

David C. Jacobsen

THE WESTMINSTER PRESS · PHILADELPHIA

LIBRARY OF CONGRESS CATALOG CARD No. 67–15870

PUBLISHED BY THE WESTMINSTER PRESS ®
PHILADELPHIA, PENNSYLVANIA

PRINTED IN THE UNITED STATES OF AMERICA

To Helen
Wife, Mother of Four,
and
Patient, Trusting Critic

1455066

Contents

Preface

The purpose of this volume is to open a conversation. It contains some of the results of a struggle for identity through about twenty years of work in the church. Some of the material is from the depths of my soul. Some of it is perhaps superficial. All of it has some base in experience.

The volume is addressed to whoever will read it. Perhaps it could be termed "an open letter." Those who are frustrated and those who are curious may find in it something that is helpful and interesting. The objective is limited, but there are here some things that are not discussed in other books and places.

The young man who considers the possibility of service in the ministry can see here how at least one man considers his calling. The middle-aged man who is still struggling (and all of us are) may find something to alleviate his anxiety or to make him angry. The layman may find some insight into the role of the clergyman that will help him to understand and relate to this strange breed. At any rate, he may be able to find a topic for genuine conversation.

One category of concern is completely passed over. It is a consideration of what the role does to the man. Any minister who carries an image for ten or twenty years will be shaped to some degree by the expectations of others. He becomes a type. This is frequently a sad fact. Old friends who see a man after he has spent ten years in the ministry may find him sharply cynical or smoothly professional. They will seldom find him to be the same man. There is also a shocking moment when the professional minister hears himself speaking and suddenly recognizes the change in himself.

All of this is the other side of the coin. The professional does not operate in a vacuum, and he does not escape without being deeply affected by the responsibility he has assumed. He is particularly affected by the expectations of others.

This book is not a defense of the present structure of congregational life in the Protestant churches in the United States. There is abundant evidence that this whole structure should be reexamined, disassembled, and hopefully reshaped. There is need for a new appreciation of the priesthood of all, and a recognition that the present structure of the church is responsible for much of its own paralysis.

However, the old forms *will* be with us for a long time to come. Social institutions change slowly. Religious institutions have higher viscosity than most. Therefore, we are faced with the fact of a structure and, with that structure, the role of the minister. This role is filled with ambiguities and pains.

The ministerial role does have, however, certain positive aspects and uses. It is not all bad, even though there is great anxiety about the role among the Protestant ministers of this generation. There is frequent rejection of it, especially among graduates of the more sophisticated theological seminaries. They feel it improper for any such role to be foisted off upon them by society.

The young minister is irritated at the hypocrisy displayed by a parishioner when he apologizes, " Sorry, Rev.," after allowing some common Anglo-Saxon phrase to slip through his speech filter. The minister is hurt at being regarded as a third sex (men, women, and clergymen). He can expect to get details of female surgery that would make a strong sailor blush. It is a matter of little consequence but it gives him a consciousness of the role in which he has been cast by his profession. It is this which grates on him. A good deal of his pipe-smoking and cocktail-sipping is a deliberate effort to get out of his role. The sweetest music he hears is the voice of a respected parishioner telling him, " You don't really seem like a minister at all."

The contention of these pages will be that this role has positive values. We simply waste a valuable foothold when we try to "kick the role" by displaying a worldliness. This tends to sacrifice the purchase that might be had if the role could be used as a base for mutual growth.

There is a positive way to *use* the role. Deliberate destruction of this image in the minds of others has negative consequences, but humble, intelligent exploitation of the role can give an opening for its constructive reinterpretation. Out-and-out denial of the " role " simply contributes to the already over-flowing reservoir of misunderstanding.

Two problems ask for comment. Much of what is said is to be, I hope, responsive to these questions: First, what is the role of the minister in the mind of the beholder? Second, how can the discomfort and irritation resulting from the knowledge of " what others see in me " be used in positive ways?

My purpose is not to go over the same territory in which so many have been reading and thinking for the past few years. (Let us grant that authenticity, congruency, personhood, and self are all valid goals for us to pursue as human beings.) Our function here is to consider the problem of dealing with an area that is much more concrete, that of our professional role. This is an area which is elusive enough because we are dealing with subjective matter in other people's heads. But it *is* a far easier thing than the mysterious realm of the search for self.

It is appropriate to acknowledge debts in this context. They are legion, and most of them will never be paid. A host of patient parishioners would come at the head of the list. Many fellow ministers have helped to shape what is here. These persons cannot be held responsible for the errors or the prejudices that may shine through. These are mine. These friends do deserve credit for anything of value.

In particular, I would thank John D. Furnas, Th.D., Professor of Field Education at San Francisco Theological Seminary. He has been a valued counselor and helped to temper some of this material with his maturity and humanity. The session of the Sausalito Presbyterian Church has been patient and valiant in allowing experimentation and time. Perhaps most of all, thanks should go to my unusual and valued secretary, Mrs. Chalmers Donaldson, who has typed, read, commented upon, and, in places, acted as editor of this work.

Miss Jeanne Knakal, M.S.W., has brought important technical knowledge to the manuscript. The Reverend Wesley Baker, a longtime friend, has furnished, unknowingly, a great deal of inspiration. It is appropriate to thank Mr. and Mrs. Fremont B. Hitchcock, Jr. Without their generous help it would have been virtually impossible to acquire much of the experience reflected here.

D. C. J.

Sausalito, California

Chapter 1

The Concept of Role in Vocation

No man,
for any considerable period,
can wear one face to himself,
and another to the multitude,
without finally getting bewildered as to which
may be the true.

> — Nathaniel Hawthorne,
> *The Scarlet Letter* (1850).

When a person enters any vocation, he must be prepared to face a great mystery. He will be dealing with images that others associate with his vocation. These images must be dealt with *in addition* to all the other dynamics of personal relationships. Essentially, this amounts to dealing with the fact of prejudice in the minds of a man's associates. This prejudice is inevitable and unpredictable.

The eyes that view the professional are informed by sources over which that professional has little or no control. It is possible for those eyes to be taught by fiction, rumor, or fact. Frequently, they are conditioned by all of these, and the burden of image is always present. It may be a flattering image or a derogatory one. The possibility of the image's having a base in reality is remote. Our concern in these pages is directed particularly to the minister and his image. It is appropriate to begin with the clear acceptance that every profession has its image.

The medical doctor is forced to deal with a composite image made up of material gathered at random by the beholder. He may carry himself with quiet humility, but in the eyes of his neighbor or his patient, he may wear the halo of Tom Dooley or Dr. Livingstone. His patient has seen Ben Casey and Dr. Kildare on television. He has read articles in the *Reader's Digest* about the latest medical discoveries, and picked up *The Saturday Evening Post* and discovered articles about hospitals' overcharging, and perhaps even articles that question the ethical standards of this profession. He remembers stories about the time his mother called a doctor in a crisis and none would come. He has heard someone refer to the unwillingness of a medical man to stop at the scene of an accident. The composite of all these impressions represents the image with which the medical doctor must deal. Since he is dealing with the patient as a professional, he is bound to a limited time span. He cannot subject his patient to a projective test and thus discover the prejudices which give nuances to all that the doctor may say. There is neither time nor justification for such a test.

Within the limits he occupies, he must do the best he can with what he suspects lies hidden in the dark recesses of his patient's mind. If he feels that his image has the weight of authority, he may try to use that authority constructively. It may be possible for him to use it to advantage when prescribing an essential diet. That same authority may prove a source of pain and anxiety if he faces responsibility for a patient with an incurable disease. The problem to be solved by the physician is how to use the image constructively.

Another of the classic professions that carries with it an image is that of the attorney. We are all laymen to one another. The man who has not "studied law" or "passed the bar" is a layman to the attorney. The client may carry in his mind the same complicated, preconceived idea of who the attorney really is and what his professional status really means.

Here again it is a composite of all the varied experiences, moldy jokes, adages, and superficial judgments that make up the total subjective image. He may have exaggerated ideas of the capabilities of his lawyer or he may have deep suspicion of all lawyers. He has watched Perry Mason and he has heard about Jake Ehrlich and Melvin Belli. There is also the historical image of Clarence Darrow and William Jennings Bryan. So, there is a combination of faith and suspicion that dwells in the recesses of the client's mind. Here again the problem is the same. How does the lawyer use the image in creative ways? If he carries the image of authority, he can offer comfort to his innocent client. If he carries the image of a shyster, he may stimulate the conscience of a guilty client. Either of these may be a legitimate and creative use of his image and role. But whether he likes it or not, he carries the image.

The image that is carried by the minister is likewise a potential burden or a potential asset. He is expected to be " good." He may be expected to be wise in esoteric areas of theology and Bible and literature. He is at times credited with a vast range of authority (frequently about things that do not really seem to matter). By some, it is assumed that he will be an impractical dreamer. He is assigned the category of saint, junior grade, and is asked to be particularly good. The picture of the minister in our culture, the portrait of the minister in history and literature, on stage or screen, in radio and television all contribute to this image. Billy Sunday, Norman Vincent Peale, Fulton Sheen, and the evangelist with whom a parishioner had contact as a child — all these tend to contribute to the image carried by the minister. The image is influenced by generalized ideas gathered from the impressions of a Jewish rabbi, a Catholic priest, or any variety of Protestant clergy. The impression left by ministers who serve in the same community or by predecessors in a particular pulpit all have their impress upon the burden that must be carried by an individual pastor.

If he is " good," he is frequently resented and invariably kept at arm's length by some of his contemporaries. If he fails to fulfill his assignment to be " good," he can become an excuse for their failures. Not only this, but if he fails to be " good," he may be heaped with projected hostility and contempt by those who handle their own guilt in this way.

Society tends to operate on double standards — one standard for the minister and one for the rest of society. The " goodness " of society is sometimes expected to be acted out by the minister. This frequently applies only to simple and meaningless types of goodness. If a man is brave enough to risk his person in a really relevant witness to justice in a civil rights program, or if he adopts a firm stance on some social issue, he may find the image misinterpreted again. He may be welcome to stand for " goodness " in areas that are irrelevant. He is welcome to "not smoke " and "not drink " vicariously. But he is seldom welcome to stand for social justice vicariously in the same way.

These conceptions are frequently accentuated in the minds of younger ministers and prove burdensome. They imply an irrelevance and a shallowness that degrade the person along with the office. Most men enter the ministry in the hope that they will make a lasting contribution to society, and irrelevance is a cause for pain. In addition, the drive toward authenticity and congruency puts a man out of joint. The vocation and the man should somehow be wedded. Blizzard puts it this way:

"The problem of the minister in the local church is to develop an image of himself that is congenial with his theological orientation, that adequately explains his function in the church, and that permits him to be related effectively to all personnel in the social system. The general image that the people have of the clergy in our culture, and the socialization that they have toward the clergy through previous social interaction, are a part of the parish context into which a minister must fit whether he is a novice in the profession or a person of long experience. The minister's self-image is a major factor in the situation." [1]

It is this problem to which we address ourselves.

Chapter 2

The Ministry as a Profession

Let me at this point draw a distinction between role relation-
ships and interpersonal relationships — a distinction which is
often overlooked in the current spate of literature that has to
do with human relations. Roles are inescapable. They must be
played or else the social system will not work. A role by defini-
tion is a repertoire of behavior patterns which must be rattled
off in appropriate contexts, and all behavior which is irrelevant
to the role must be suppressed. But what we often forget is the
fact that it is a person *who is playing the role. This person has*
a self, or, I should say, he is *a self. All too often the roles that*
a person plays do not do justice to all of his self. In fact, there
may be nowhere that he may just be *himself. Even more, the*
person may not know *his self. He may, in Horney's (1950)*
terms, be self-alienated. This fascinating term, "self-aliena-
tion," means that an individual is estranged from his real self.
His real self becomes a stranger, a feared and distrusted
stranger. Estrangement and alienation from one's real self, is at
the root of the "neurotic personality of our time" so eloquently
described by Horney (1936).

— Sidney M. Jourard, *The Transparent Self:*
Self-disclosure and Well-being (D. Van
Nostrand Company, Inc., 1964), pp. 22–23.

Ambivalence as a Clerical Syndrome

Within the ministry, there is a high degree of discontent, confusion, and questioning about the role. Part of the source of tension is the search on the part of the minister for his own selfhood. There is a healthy yearning for authenticity among the clergy, and the role that is placed on him is a major source of stress. It is hard work to remain hidden in the role, because it means that each response must to some degree be calculated. If he struggles to keep himself unknown to others, he will suffer from debilitating and destructive stress. The construction of a false image which is then played out before the public on a round-the-clock basis is dangerous. Students of psychosomatic medicine in recent years have pointed this out very specifically. The asthmatic, the ulcer patient, the person suffering from migraine headaches may be suffering under the stress of incongruency. He may be unable to correlate the image with the self.

A part of this is due to the mistaken understanding of the nature of the church and the vocation of the ministry. The ministry is regarded by some as a special sacred calling to a holy vocation within a mystical and pure community called the church. It is this idea in the mind of a young minister as he prepares for his work which is frequently doomed to quick and jarring disappointment. Many men are jarred initially by their experience at the theological seminary. They anticipate a community of mutually concerned and compassionate students and faculty. When they arrive, they find a group of ordinary human beings with the same problems that other people have. Their new colleagues are not much holier, frequently less holy, than the ordinary people at home or in college.

For some who may have been nurtured through the years as seminary students, the grinding shock may come with the first parish. Here again are ordinary people. "Not only is my job not what I thought it would be but the Christian community falls short. Here I am, interested in counseling and in teaching, and I am stuck with administration and meetings, and a stubborn session and a bunch of old-fashioned deacons."

When a man is faced with this reality in the parish, he is frequently shaken very deeply. It may be useful to remember Paul's view of himself as an " earthenware jar " containing the "priceless treasure" of resurrection witness. This same metaphor is applicable to the church, " an earthenware jar," easily shattered, not particularly attractive, and without luster. Yet this secular community, this earthenware jar, contains the "priceless treasure" of resurrection witness. Moreover, this body of semibelievers may be essential to God's purpose. Certainly, it is important. Assuredly, it is old. How can a man be reconciled to work within this church?

In dealing with the problem of the earthiness of the church, a man may call up important realities. First of all, the church remains the most significant single witness to the resurrection. If we really do live in a resurrection world, people should be told. The church may not be working very hard at its task, but it continues the most important witness to the resurrection.

Secondly, the church is no worse than other secular institutions. Sometimes it even seems to be healthier and more forgiving. At times it is motivated by human concern. People are still healed through its ministry.

Thirdly, the church shows signs of resurrection in our generation. There are visible facts on the horizon. It may be that our lifetime will see the old body raised from the dead. Certainly, the involvement of the church in the civil rights struggle, modest though that involvement might be, is indication of life. There are signs that old wounds are being healed and the scattered brethren are being drawn together again. It is critical that the ecumenical movement be of sufficient depth that it be a resurrection and not just a union. There is no reason to believe that God can use a large corpse more efficiently than several small ones. But the ecumenical movement does hold promise.

Fourthly, and most important of all, the ministry, even in

a far from perfect church, offers opportunity for vital human contact. The potential channels for this contact in the church are made vital by the secular nature of the encounter into which the minister is drawn. Skill and calculation will be required, but the role can be used creatively.

A second source of ambivalence among men in the ministry is that produced by the role. It is not fair for a man to be forever burdened by having other people think they know who he is when they only know his vocation. The minister is actually a professional. He can accept the fact that all professions carry an image in the minds of others. Those professions have to make use of their image. The minister should make use of his image instead of allowing others to use it, and he should do so without guilt.

The concept of the professional is not that of a person who acts out an image for the public twenty-four hours a day. A minister can retain his integrity and proper self-identity at the same time that he carries his role with professional concern for the good of those to whom he ministers. There is no reason for him to feel guilty for carrying himself with professional competence. There is no reason why his professional role needs to be mixed with his self-image in a destructive way. He has the same problem of self-acceptance as other people have. If he is to be healthy, he must accept the dark side of his self along with the light. But he need not claim to be all light. It is dangerous for him to do so.

Complaints about low salaries, long hours, or drafty manses are set aside if the vocation seems to be relevant and useful. It can be relevant and useful if approached with calculated care. "The Church is something like Noah's ark. If it weren't for the storm outside, you couldn't stand the smell inside." (A late medieval manuscript, quoted by Robert McAfee Brown.) [2]

This is not a sentimental picture, nor is it calculated to be such, but it may be realistic enough to appeal to our generation. Certainly we are aware of a "storm outside." The quarrel which we might pick with the old manuscript is that the church does not stink on the inside. It is just a secular organization. The odor is no more prominent in the church than it is in the bank or in the legislature. It is just that so many expect to smell roses instead of city streets.

The Concept of Profession

Each of the classic professions — medicine, law, and the church — carries an implicit profession of faith. The very word " profession " has significance because it implies a *pro*-fession of faith in some person or concept.

The man of medicine professes his faith in the healing arts. If he is a modern medical doctor, he has professed his faith in the methods of modern surgery and drug therapy. If he is a psychiatrist, he operates on the basis of a faith in some system of values, or some concept of personal dynamics which are essentially objects of faith. He may act upon that professional faith in various ways. He may disavow the validity of drug therapy or turn from surgery or from psychiatry as legitimate modes of treatment. But he, nevertheless, has entered a *pro*-fession and as such has professed his faith in some aspects of the art.

If he is loyal to the profession, he will defend and protect others of the same profession. It may be suspected by the cynical that the protective attitude is rooted in fears of financial loss or loss of prestige. At the base, however, it is a loyalty to the profession. A stated faith in the tools and methods of that profession is implied by acceptance of the professional status.

The lawyer is an officer of the court. His basic profession of faith, from a vocational view, is toward the state and the system of law which operates in the state. He is required to act upon that faith. He must operate with faith in the judges and the courts. He must have a belief in the validity of the constitution, and, with certain limitations, a faith in his fellow attorneys.

The clergyman is a professional also. His profession, he

might say, is to Almighty God. But I would postulate that his basic profession of faith *as a clergyman* or *as a minister* is to the *visible church.*

If he is to be a professional within the visible structure of the church, he must have some faith that the structure has a valid status and useful function. He must believe that the visible body of believers which is gathered into the church has purpose and is worthy of his support and the expenditure of his labor. As he grows older — and wiser, we hope — he may see the flaws of that visible structure more vividly each year. This may make him less sure about the validity of the claim upon him from the visible church. If this should take place, he ought to examine himself to see if he is still capable of making the profession of faith in the visible body and remaining a *professional.* If he can no longer see the role of the visible body as legitimate, he should retool for some profession that is now valid under his reeducated system of values.

It seems inappropriate for a man who has lost the faith to remain in the profession of the ministry he formerly professed. Certainly we would feel that it was inappropriate for a lawyer to continue to practice law if he had lost faith in the Constitution, or the system of law. Equally, we would reject the doctor who continued to practice medicine after having cynically rejected the methods of medicine.

Now, certainly the clergyman is not required to profess and maintain a faith in the church as it is currently structured. He is not required to do this any more than a doctor is prevented from advancing the state of the art through research, or the lawyer prohibited from the exercise of his franchise as a voter. Men who entered the profession of medicine thirty years ago find themselves professing a faith in a discipline completely different today from the one they entered. The clergyman is committed to change the church's structure, by orderly means, into a church "without spot or blemish." He is, however, also committed to the validity of the called-out, called-together community of believers. He may be sophisticated about the depth and meaning of the belief of that community, and he may have reservations about the effectiveness of the church's program. But he does not doubt that the church should exist. He cannot be a cynic and sit in arrogant judgment over that church and still remain a responsible professional.

He may recognize that the church is an earthenware jar. It is easy to break, and less than perfect in every way, but he does not reject it. The clergyman works within the secular organization. This may seem a narrow definition. The protest could be made that the minister is called to a deeper loyalty than simply to the visible church. This is certainly true. We are all called to a deeper loyalty than to the visible church. We are called to place our faith in God alone rather than in the visible body of believers. The minister is likewise called to this deeper faith as a person. But as a minister (as a professional) within the visible body he is called to have faith in that visible body. If he leaves the profession of the ministry, this does not necessarily mean that he has left his basic faith. It is possible to be a Christian and yet lack faith in the legitimacy of the visible body.

This concept of the ministry as a profession among others may be freedom-producing for some and anxiety-producing for others. Many have felt their calling to be of a different nature. If the minister is involved in a vocation that calls him to loyalty to the visible body of believers, then he has a tangible task. This should be freedom-producing. It is also anxiety-producing because there are times when a man's understanding of God's purpose and love conflicts with the " good " of the institution.

Every clergyman must make decisions that affect the good or the growth of the institution. There are times when the growth of the institution is made at the expense of human values which the body of Christ is instructed to consider as primary values. The minister must then consider the meaning of his vocation. He is called to express his faith in the visible body. He therefore must consider the institution as a valid expression of the body. Theoretically the numerical strength of the institution and the financial security of the congregation ought not to be considered. At least they should not be considered as primary. Yet they are facts of life.

A certain Machiavellian character then rests upon the clergyman as he makes decisions. He must base those decisions on an ethic which is dynamic and calculated to be the most loving expression possible. The total good of the most persons must be considered. The pastor must make decision as to what will serve the body and the purpose of God for the body. If he knows the congregation to be immature and incapable of absorbing the impact of a decision that is too radically loving toward one person, he may decide for the good of the institution.

This statement has an ugly ring about it. It brings to mind the rationalization of the Pharisees that it is "expedient . . . that one man should die" (John 11:50). Nevertheless, the pastor is continually faced with this dilemma. He must make separation between the one and the many. It is not appropriate for him to make every choice in deference to the many. This is a neglect of his responsibility before God as a pastor. But it is necessary for him to make *some* choices that neglect the needs of single individuals or small groups. Of all the conflicts in which the pastor is trapped, this is the most critical. Illustration: A staff member in the church has offended the neurotic wife of a leading elder. The pastor and others work to establish some reconciliation but fail. The session is faced with the necessity of either discharging the staff member or offending a family of long-standing influence in the church. The question of who is right becomes somewhat academic in a situation of this nature. It is impossible to assume that men and women in the ruling body are without feelings. They have their own limitations and carry these into any decision. The pastor, who moderates the session, must decide whether he will go along with the conclusion which may do real damage to a person or to a group. Actually, he cannot avoid the decision or the hurt that will result no matter what may be decided. If, after careful study, he decides that the values are weighted in that way, he must conclude for the good of the many. If the church is " sacred body of Christ," it should act as that body. It should respond as an organism with love toward all the parties to the conflict. But the fact is that the church is not a sacred organism. It is a secular institution. It may not respond in love. It may, and frequently does, respond as other institutions respond. It may respond with defensiveness and a passion for self-preservation. Should the pastor tolerate this sort of response at the expense of an individual? If he is committed to the visible institution, as a professional, then he can respond with calculated and educated calm. It may be very painful for him to do so. But his professional responsibility is more important. If he believes that he is a special shepherd assigned by the call of God to a special " sacred body of Christ" which must always act as an organism, then he may collapse from the pain.

This is not an exaggerated illustration of a case. There is a continuing series of such choices faced by the pastor. They are inevitable and they are painful. If the pastor learns to make decisions in this agonizing impasse without pangs, then he has grown hardened and lost his humanity. If, on the other hand, he hesitates too long, laboring between two unhappy choices, he has abdicated his professional responsibility. Others will make the decision. Even so, the decision will cut and hurt those who are involved.

The minister is called to a task that is essential to the institution. He is called to be a competent professional and not a sentimental perfectionist. He must be sensitive to need and the group dynamic that cuts across the visible body to the injury of some. But the sensitivity ought not to paralyze him.

A Resurrection Faith

Two facets of faith must be present in the minister. He must believe in the resurrection and he must have faith in the church. He must believe in resurrection because, if he does not, he will have nothing to preach and his ministry will be without meaning. He must believe in the church because this is the tool which he is committed to use as a professional.

The resurrection is central to the Christian faith. The everlasting meaning of Jesus who gives himself in love to the world and is crucified is specific. He is telling us in that act that love is dangerous. If Jesus was raised from the dead, then love has meaning and we live in a universe in which love is ultimate value. If he was not raised from the dead, we live in a world of absurdity where the safest thing to do is to love no one at all. The sensible way to live in a world that kills love is to watch out for yourself and for no one else.

The manner of the resurrection is a matter of much debate and will never be settled. The fact of resurrection is a matter of faith and will never be supported by scientific evidence. The fact remains that either we live in a universe where resurrection took place and is possible, or we do not live in such a world. Either we are candidates for resurrection, or we are not candidates. If we are not, then the world is a dangerous place where we are foolish to be good or to love. If we are candidates, then every decision we make should be influenced by that fact.

Resurrection is not confined to life after visible death. Resurrection is the renewal of life in daily loss. It is the renewal of life even in situations which involve hard choices between the one and the many. Those who are hurt can still be raised to new and useful life.

Nothing is more certain in life than the fact of loss. We all suffer from loss. We lose money, we lose loved ones, all of us will eventually lose our youth. The gray hairs and the wrinkles come, our bodies grow less attractive and weaker and we must deal with the loss. Paul said, "Loss is gain!" When we lose the things we cling to, they open the way for resurrection. This does not mean that loss should not be resisted or that pain is not real or that death is not a fact. It does mean that creative life can come out of loss as Christ came from the grave.

If Paul's contention that "loss is gain" has validity, then it means that we live in a world where God's creative life is never frustrated by hatred or death. Conversely, if we live in a world where "loss is loss," then we have lots of evidence of the triumph of evil and hatred and death. The minister is able to give this kind of interpretation of the resurrection to both parties in a conflict.

Even a minister who believes in resurrection will not allow this belief to influence his decisions all the time. We all live as agnostics. If we really believed without question that God is love and that love is the supreme fact of life, we would base our decisions in that love. But we believe this only a little bit. For some, it is only a suspicion. For others, the resurrection truth becomes a part of their total stance in life.

There will be times in the professional life of a minister when his faith is less than a burning brand. His humanity will ensure this fact. A crisis demands his ministry, and he himself may be filled with doubt. When this happens, as it inevitably will, in the life of a clergyman, he is bound by his loyalty to Christ and the church and by his concern for the people to whom he ministers. He is bound to say what is appropriate in the moment by way of witness. He can and must give witness to the resurrection even though his spirit is cold. This is his responsibility as a professional.

This means that in his ministry to the Christian community, this should be his supreme witness. The community should be willing to sacrifice part of its life for the sake of the individual within it. This should be the thrust of its witness. However, if it does not act in this faith, the individual who has been hurt or rejected is still able to respond in creative ways on the basis of faith in the resurrection. Even though the visible church has set aside resurrection truth, the individual Christian is not excluded from that faith. The true professional minister will attempt to interpret this truth both to the body of the church and to the individual.

Real ambivalence exists in the minds of a vast number of ministers. This is particularly true of the younger clergymen. There is doubt about the usefulness of the visible church and there is irritation at the role that must be carried. The first doubt can be set aside only by faith that God is still using the "earthenware jar" of the church. The second doubt is helped by the application of the concept of profession to the ministry. The application of this concept is both liberating and frightening. The concept of profession as it is applied to the ministry can be inferred to be a potentially callousing experience. It ought not to be so. The ministry is inevitably a series of painful decisions. These decisions are often the choices between the good of the church as an institution and the comfort of an individual. The minister as a professional is forced to participate in these decisions. He can participate as a believing Christian only if he has a resurrection faith himself. The thrust of his ministry to both the church community and to the individuals who make it up must always be determined by this concept of resurrection truth.

Chapter 3

Responses to the Fact of Role

I hope you have not been leading a double life, pretending to be wicked, and being really good all the time. That would be hypocrisy.

— Oscar Wilde, *The Importance of Being Earnest*, Act II.

It is possible for a man to take his role and image with absolute seriousness. A man can sell his soul in order to establish himself in a particular category. The person who follows this pathway toward his vocational integrity will find himself adapting to the environment. This will be full of problems because often he will not be able to assess what is expected of him. This is a tremendously confusing and difficult response to make. If a man tries to conform to the preconceived notions of people around him, he is faced with the task, first of all, of finding out what those preconceived ideas really are. This is very difficult to do.

Even after finding out, he must decide whether the image in his parishioner's mind is positive or negative. That is, he must decide whether or not it is considered by the parishioner to be good or bad. Then, having reached a conclusion here, he must proceed to act in such a way as to confirm the positive aspects of the role and mitigate or deny by his action its negative aspects.

Finding out what another believes and then conforming to that notion is very complex. As a man attempts to live within such a process, he finds that each decision offers enough choices to ensure a fair percentage of error. In the end, the er- rors will compound and come crashing in upon him. The vision of a man trying constantly to please others is not pleasant. It is even less pleasant when his efforts are doomed to failure from the very beginning. He is faced with an impossible task. He may see evidence of rejection in innocent responses — re- sponses that are perfectly neutral. He may find himself assign- ing tremendous significance to relatively innocuous signs on the part of the person whom he is trying to please. It would not be an exaggeration to say that the person who attempts to conform in the way described above is taking a shortcut to paranoia.

Rogers comments that the deepest drive that comes to the fore in his counselees is a passion for selfhood. Choosing other than the real self is the pathway to despair. The drive toward authenticity is the drive toward mental and emotional health. To deny this drive expression and to attempt conformity to outside pressure is dangerous enough. To do all of this without a clear knowledge of the content to which a man is attempting to conform is even more dangerous. Conformity may appear to be a comfortable solution. In the end it will become less com- fortable. For the really sensitive person, it will be not only uncomfortable but impossible. Nevertheless, some men take this pathway. They may do so because of some mystical idea about a " call." They may do so because they have confused the church with a parental authority figure. This kind of iden- tity is not unknown. They may do so because no one has ever convinced them that they are professionals.

It is possible, also, to attempt to hide within the role. There is a certain security which is a tempting trap. The role can be insulation from pain of involvement. No one exposes the whole person. It is far too frightening to be that vulnerable. We hide behind an image or a persona which is projected toward those with whom we have to do. This means that those persons and their reactions are predictable to us within certain limits.

The role of the minister offers a shelter to the sensitive spirit. It is a shelter that is almost impregnable, if he plays the role with sufficient skill. It is possible to develop a series of pat, stereotyped phrases that can be brought up out of the memory and can fit almost any situation. If a man has learned his theological lessons well, he can answer all kinds of painful questions that are posed by life. He can answer them out of his bag of tricks. If he wishes to do so, it is possible, in this way, to avoid the pains of real human encounter. He need simply throw up the "theological answer."

One of the perpetual pains of the ministry is found in the problem of pain itself. The unanswered and unanswerable problem of theology is the problem of pain. A terminal cancer patient asks in real pain for the answer to the question: Why? Why does God allow this to happen to me?

To this kind of question there are all sorts of theological answers that sound profound. They were learned by the minister in seminary. They have some theoretical validity, and as such they deserve some degree of respect from us. But they are not existential answers. They do not speak to the person in pain. The minister can choose these answers or he can choose a different pathway. He can identify with the patient. There is no satisfactory answer to the problem of pain. The minister, standing beside the bed, can even admit this to the patient and in this way enter into that person's world of pain to some degree. At the same time that a minister confesses this humanity, it is appropriate to make a profession of faith. Even when he cannot *feel* the resurrection reality, the minister is called upon to bear witness to that reality. He can do this even while he suffers from inward pain which is all but unbearable. He can and must do this when he feels no elation whatsoever. It is his professional responsibility to share this most precious of all truths with the person who needs it most. If the New Testament teaches anything at all, it teaches that good can come from pain. As Jesus was crucified and raised from the dead, so love that is rejected or pain that has no visible meaning can be raised by God to give creative life. Loss is gain. Somehow, no matter how he may feel, the minister must say this. He may do so by word or deed or silence, but his professional responsibility is as a witness.

It is a dual pathway. Identity with pain and the person suffering pain must be real. Such identity can be an emotional confession of finitude which can be therapeutic to the patient. But the simple witness is also essential. The minister does not do anyone a real service by abdicating his role to the degree that he has no theology. Neither is it necessary for him to suffer from pangs of guilt because he does not subjectively feel the reality of the witness which he is attempting to convey. He is not God. He is a man with professional responsibility.

It is not necessary to claim firsthand knowledge of the resurrection. It is necessary to make a statement of faith that resurrection is real, that God raised Jesus from the dead, and that we are candidates for resurrection ourselves. But this is a statement of faith. It will always remain a statement of faith. The degree of emotional involvement that a man feels in relation to his witness is not the critical thing. The witness may have healing effect, even when it is spoken with mechanical precision and little emotional conviction. The witness should be supported by confidence that has roots in experiences of the past. It cannot always have those roots, but it will always be a witness.

Real human involvement remains an essential ingredient in the ministry of any man. The minister's humanity and his identity with the person who suffers is always a source of pain. The man who identifies completely with the role has stepped into a dangerous category. If he is asked to answer questions such as those above, i.e., the problem of pain, he may feel that it is essential for his answers to be correct. If he is willing to recognize himself as a man and a professional, he can still have the privilege of being wrong. The word " professional " is used

here in what is hoped to be a positive sense. There is a use of
the word that is negative also. To be a professional in this sense
may imply a callousness and sophistication. It is possible that
the man who is the most professional in the negative connotation of that word is in reality the most sensitive. It may be
that his "professional" attitude is a means of insulating himself from intolerable pain. Complete identity with the role as
it is envisaged in the minds of others may be an abdication of
humanity. The professional is able to admit his humanity, make
his witness, and continue to live.

Balance must be maintained between human sensitivity
which gives usefulness to a man's work and the insulation
which makes it possible for him to exist. It is not necessary
that a minister be comfortable or free from the pain of involvement at all times. Neither is it necessary for him to be rubbed
so raw by direct contact that he cannot do anything but feel.
He must use his professional sense to determine the extent of
his human involvement.

There is no reason why a man cannot quote, "Weep with
those who weep," and yet function as a clear-headed professional. It requires skill and care to do this, but it can be done.
The danger lies in the total adoption of the insulation of pro-
fessionalism. It is easier for a man to take the pathway toward
comfort. This is especially true for the man with a large parish responsibility. He may not wish to retreat from the feeling
level. But the demands of numbers make it impossible to share
humanity deeply with all at all times.

The ministry calls a man into deep and human involvement.
The pains of that involvement can overwhelm a man. It is only
proper for him to have some kind of insulation. Not only must
this insulation be available for himself but for the sake of
those to whom he owes a ministry in the moment. This is what
is meant by the attitude of the professional.

There will be times when a pastor is called to minister to
those in crisis and loss when he can say nothing at all. He may
literally weep with those who weep. This may be all he can

do in the moment. Nevertheless, he has a time later when he can give a more rational ministry. Suppose he is called to the house of a young couple who are complete strangers to him. The father has just backed his car out of the garage and run over his three-year-old girl. The mortician has called in the young pastor to help. The dynamics of this situation are terribly complex. There is the young father's feeling of guilt. There is the desperation of the young mother. There are the shallow, half-forgotten lessons of Sunday school which are being hastily recalled. No one is articulate enough to touch the depth of feeling. No superficial talk will help. But a man can weep. He can weep at the moment, but the minister must remain sufficiently in control of himself so that he can return for a useful ministry at a later time.

Suppose the minister is called to the scene of a disaster. A plane crashes in a schoolyard and forty children are killed or injured. He may spend half a day going from hospital to hospital, trying to get families together. He must relate and communicate with the staff of the school and of the hospital, with the parents, the desperate teachers, and the dying children. He must relate to frustrated doctors and nurses, and all of this in a rush. There is no time to weep. His task is different here and it is an essential work which no one else is able to do at that moment. His weeping may be delayed until he sits some evening, days later, at the supper table with his family. It may come then as a shaking flood and be the means of soothing the raw surface of his deep involvement. But if he is a professional, he can and must remain rational in the crises.

A rational humanity is demanded of the pastor and if he has adopted his role too seriously, and taken the expectations of others as his prime guide, he cannot fulfill this passion-filled category. There is pain in the ministry. If there is no pain, there is less than a ministry. But the pain must belong to the self. And the self is human. It is not an image produced in the mind of someone else. No image to which a minister is attempting to conform can carry pain.

Rejection of the Role

There is a tendency on the part of some ministers to try to set aside any semblance of role and to be *self alone*. This attempt is expressed among some by chain-smoking or cocktail-drinking. The telling of off-color jokes is inferred to be a means of confessing one's humanity and freedom from convention. It really becomes quite bizarre if the man who persists in this masquerade insists on wearing clerical garb. At one time, he is saying two things. By his actions, he may be attempting to be divorced from all others in his profession and to effect a casual disregard for tradition or image. By his garb, he may be giving an indication of his direct relation to long church tradition. As a matter of fact, the incongruity may be the source of some of the "humor" in his jokes. "Do you know where I heard this story? You wouldn't believe I heard it from a minister."

A great deal of confusion can result when a man tries to deal with his role by the tactic of direct rejection. There is confusion in the minds of parishioners and others who witness this. They may have a real yearning to call upon this pastor for some sort of help. If a pastor expresses a casual cynicism in his attitude, this may make it possible for the parishioner to see him as thoroughly human. At the same time, it may also cut him off completely from the possibility of professional usefulness. When a man says to the minister, "You don't seem like a minister at all," it may be music to the ears of a frustrated pastor. It may mean something deeper. It may mean, "I feel you are a human friend but I will have to take my deeper needs elsewhere to discuss them." It may even mean, "I wish I could find someone, somewhere, who is willing to be a stable point in my surroundings." It may reflect a simple yearning after someone who is willing to assume the category of professional in the horizon of that particular parishioner.

John Updike in his book *Rabbit, Run* describes a young Episcopal clergyman trying to make contact with a confused young man. The clergyman tries on the golf course, by total acceptance, by availability, and so forth, to relate to the young man. He never condemns the youth even though he is a thoroughly irresponsible person who has accepted the responsibilities of marriage and family and failed to fulfill them. The tactic does not work, and toward the middle of the book the young priest goes to see the Lutheran pastor of the man's family. He is greeted with a barrage which withers his whole self-image.

"Do you think this is your job?" . . . says the Lutheran pastor, ". . . to meddle in these people's lives? I know what they teach you at Seminary now: this psychology and that. But I don't agree with it. You think now your job is to be an unpaid doctor, to run around and plug up the holes and make everything smooth. I don't think that. I don't think that's your job."

"I only — "

"No, now let me finish! I've been in Mount Judge twenty-seven years and you've been here two. I've listened to your story but I wasn't listening to what you said about the people, I was listening to what it said about you. What I heard was this: the story of a minister of God selling his message for a few scraps of gossip and a few games of golf. What do you think now it looks like to God, one childish husband leaving one childish wife? Do you ever think any more what God sees? Or have you grown beyond that? "

"No, of course not. But it seems to me our role in a situation like this — "

"It seems to you our role is to be cops, cops without handcuffs, without guns, without anything but our human good nature. Isn't that right? Don't answer, just think if I'm not right. Well, I say that's a Devil's idea. I say, let the cops be cops and look after their laws that have nothing to do with us." [3]

We can quarrel with the Lutheran pastor and with his narrow view of his responsibility. But he does have a certain point. There is a time when a minister is called to be a stable point in the social spectrum. He may cling so desperately to his own identity that he refuses the role. But this is not fair. He has accepted a position in the vast army of the church. He has identified with the past and is called upon to pay the price of that identity. The world is starved for stable categories. It is important for the mental and emotional health of each person that each person have some static point to which he can react. The minister may imply a moral code that the person rejects. But this does not mean that the person must be denied the possibility of placing himself over against that code. It is not comfortable to be the source of another person's feeling of guilt. When a minister enters the room, there is a tendency for conversation to change in tone. The minister may dislike the fact that he has acted as a damper. But to try to put the group at ease by denying any relation to the image that has put a damper on the conversation is a solution far too shallow. The reaction of people who will restrict their conversation in front of a minister is conditioned by a whole series of misconceptions. This is true. The act implies that God is somehow associated with the minister more directly than with others in the group. This is a sad mistake. It may also imply that ethical conduct is related to some code rather than to dynamic human encounter. It may reflect a childish understanding of right and wrong. This also is sad. It may imply that a Victorian code is thought to be more "Christian" than the earthy attitude of the Bible toward sex and life and passion. This is even more sad.

But to step out of the minister's role in this situation and to work at setting everyone at ease may be a real disservice. These three misconceptions, along with others, need some sort of interpretation and answer. The simple act of entering into conversation at the original level — or even outdoing the others in ribald jokes — may be comfortable but it may also decrease the usefulness of the minister in future situations.

Denial of the role results in confusion in the mind of the minister who does the denying. He cannot be completely divorced from the image. He may try to deny identity with it, but he will never succeed. He may only succeed in confusing everybody.

The confusion that results has already been mentioned. First, he does not know the content in the mind of the person to whom he relates. That content may be a real caricature or only a mild error. The image in the other person's mind may be one that implies a belief on the minister's part in the literal truth of the third chapter of Genesis. This may be very distasteful to him. Even so, he does not know the emotional value of the image. He does not know whether certain aspects of this subjective image reflect a positive feeling or a negative feeling.

Most important of all, the minister does not know the needs of the person he encounters. A terribly distressing thing in the ministry is evidence of a lack of sensitivity. A man may be in desperate straits and give no visible evidence. The lovely smiling face of a woman can hide a desperate alcoholic. A bluff and confident exterior can conceal a person paralyzed by fear. The minister does not know what needs really lie behind that face, and if he is always trying to set his companions at ease, he is in no position to appraise those needs.

It is possible that if he can approach the whole multiple dynamic with a professional stance, he will be able to effect some reinterpretation. He may be able to use his image in some creative way if he does not become so anxious that he paralyzes his imagination. If he is going to reinterpret his role as a professional who suffers from humanity, he should do this when he can enter into appropriate dialogue. To deny his role and attempt to affirm his humanity by the method of simply " entering in " is added confusion.

Conscious Acceptance of and Use of the Role

This brings us to the problem of dealing with the image in the minds of others in some creative way. If we have accepted the concept of the church as a secular institution and the ministry as a profession (that is, a profession of faith in the validity and usefulness of the gathered community of the church), then it should follow that the minister is free to practice his profession in the most practical way.

The concept of "the call" to the minister is a complicating factor because it tends to identify the man with the role. It is possible for a man to feel called into the ministry by a mystical call that will not be denied. This is not necessarily prominent in our culture today, but it was a factor only a generation ago. There is a sense of "individualism" attached to this idea of a mystical call which implies that the church is not a vital factor in the picture. The "call" is thought of as between God and the man who is called.

Actually, it is the church that gives validity and meaning to ordination. It is relationship to the visible, corporate body of believers that gives special character to the "called man." This ought to mean that the minister must recognize his responsible relation to the visible church and make peace with the fact that he is subject to the considered judgment of his brethren. If it is a Presbyterian relationship, he cannot remain long with the illusion that the brethren are always right. If it is to a bishop, he certainly will notice soon that the bishop is a human being. If it is a congregation to which he is subject, he could hardly be under the impression that congregational democracy is always pure and righteous. If this fallible church gives validity to the role, it is not appropriate that the role be thought of in nonutilitarian and mystical terms. The church is not always right, but it is the visible church that gives validity to the office. It should follow that the office bears a similarity to other secular professions.

How is he to accept and use the image carried by that profession? First, the minister should recognize the fact that he carries an image. He does not know its content and the content varies with the person holding that image. Even so, some aspects are similar. He is expected to be good. He is expected to be concerned. He is expected to be "spiritual" (whatever that means), and he is expected to be "acquainted with holy mystery." These may have no basis in fact but they may still constitute some of the subjective material called the image.

Secondly, having recognized the image, a minister should avoid the foolishness of kicking it. Reasons for this are indicated above, but essentially they amount to the fact that it compounds confusion already produced by the subjective residue. Take it for granted that the problem is bad enough already and that more "kicking against the goad" will only make it more confusing.

Finally, the minister is called upon to look for creative ways to use the image for constructive purposes.

There are three ways in which the minister can react to the fact of his image and role. One is to adopt that role completely and attempt to conform to what he thinks he sees in it. A second is to kick the role with vigor and attempt to be separated from it. A third and more creative use of this fact of role is to accept it, reinterpret it, and then attempt to use it in creative ways.

Chapter 4

Positive Uses of the Role

For it is Christ Jesus as Lord whom we preach, not our-
selves. . . . This priceless treasure we hold, so to speak, in
a common earthenware jar — to show that the splendid power
of it belongs to God and not to us.
— II Corinthians 4: 5, 7 (Phillips Translation).

Jesus used different approaches to different persons. When
he spoke to the woman at the well in Samaria, he was being
analytical and direct. When he taught, it was as " one who had
authority." When he drove the money changers from the
Temple, he displayed anger. When he feasted, he gave some
people the impression that he was a wine bibber, and when
he was at a party he apparently had a good time. People were
terribly confused about him. They continually attacked what
they considered to be inappropriate behavior. They called
him " Rabbi " and " Good Teacher," and he rejected these
titles. People objected because they did not know how to
take him. But he did not allow those around him to manipulate him by reference to his supposed role. He carried himself
with authenticity and he attempted continually to reinterpret
who he was. His message was conveyed by his continually
demonstrated faith in God. Surely, we have something to
learn from his attitude toward role. The lesson should help
the minister toward an acceptance of his own situation and

help him to seek out positive ways in which to use his opportunities.

No profession offers richer opportunity for a person-to-person contact than the ministry. People do come to the minister when they have troubles and problems. They may come, at times, for the wrong reasons or with the wrong expectations, but they *do* come. Other professions imply other expectations but none is more open than the ministry. The minister is available and he has a reputation for availability. Most ministers also have a reputation for being able to keep confidence. They are regarded as persons who can be trusted. Apparently, some 45 percent of all persons who seek help from a counselor go to their minister first. They go to him because he is available, because he represents authority, because he will not send a bill, and because he may have some sort of useful training and understanding of people. In addition, the minister has the opportunity to go to the person whom he wishes to contact. This is really not true of other professional groups. If a lawyer feels that it is important to talk with his client, he may telephone the client. But for the most part, he will be confined to waiting at his office for the client to take the initiative. The medical doctor is also restricted in the same way — not by physical restriction but by tradition. The social worker in some special situations has been able to go into the homes of persons in need but sometimes represents a frightening image. This is especially a problem to social workers in the Department of Public Welfare. They often have the image of the public investigator. Psychiatrists talk about pursuing their patients to their homes and, in certain restricted situations, have done so. The results of this sort of pursuit are yet to be measured. Actually, only the minister is still in a uniquely open situation, freed by tradition and, financially, by the church, to follow his own conscience in ministering to those who try to avoid him.

Dealing with Guilt

One of the most frequent motivating factors in the minds of people who come for help to a minister is the problem of guilt. When a person comes to the minister, he states his problem in different categories for the "man of God." Frequently, he comes with his mind already made up as to what is wrong and he already has in his mind a solution. The problem of guilt is frequently mentioned.

The minister has a special role in dealing with guilt. He represents authority in the field, and to most persons, he represents a "moral code." Many people have a tendency to make up their minds on moral problems with some sort of "situation ethic" as a guide. What is the most good for the most persons is a pragmatic guide to many. They do not associate the image of the minister with any such dynamic ethic, as a rule. They think of him as representing a code. They hope that the minister can help them to assess the depth of their guilt and offer them a remedy. They feel guilty and they would like to feel right again. This is a great opportunity for the reinterpretation of ethics. It is also one of the very complex problems of the minister who deals with sensitive people. But before discussing this question further, let us look at another problem encountered frequently by the clergyman.

Often the minister is approached with the hope that he will give some kind of justification for what the person has already decided to do. It is necessary for him to listen carefully if he is going to avoid some sort of prior absolution for an act that may still be in the future. It may be the best solution for a man to divorce his wife and marry his secretary. But the minister who is drawn into this sort of counsel should at least know to what he has given the nod. We hear what we wish to hear and ought not to blame the parishioner for hearing what he may wish to hear in the comments of the minister. Anyone who has been related to the pastorate or involved in pastoral counseling for any length of time can recognize the real depth of some leading generalized questions.

If a minister carries the authority that can release another from guilt, he should at least be aware of what is being sanctioned. The generalized nature of preaching and the gap that exists between pulpit and pew is an invitation to find rationale for a great host of actions. The minister who believes that his role does not really carry authority is being naïve. That authority is frequently employed by those who wish to use it for their own subjective purposes.

Dealing with guilt that has already been established in a person and is fomenting a painful anxiety is also a task for the minister. A sense of guilt is probably the most frequent motivating factor in the minds of people who come to him for help. If he is going to deal with this opportunity creatively, he must learn to separate real guilt from neurotic guilt. Real guilt does exist. And real guilt should bring a man to confession and restitution and, we would hope, to peace. Neurotic guilt also exists. Frequently, it is exaggerated out of all proportion to its basic importance. It needs to be dealt with in a different way altogether from real guilt. O. Hobart Mowrer has stated emphatically that all guilt is real guilt. He believes that no such thing as neurotic guilt exists. He chides the minister for his failure to accept the responsibility for dealing with the guilt by using appropriate theological and sacramental tools. Mowrer feels that the church has failed to accept its real role as the legal guardian of the mentally ill. He feels that the medical doctor is not the appropriate person to deal with mental illness but that the minister is the appropriate individual. By throwing out the category of neurotic guilt, Mowrer completely alters the treatment of mental illness. He has flattered the church and religion by implying that its old categories are valid and that the confusing new categories of psychology are to be ignored. The problem is that the truth lies somewhere in between. Most certainly the church has failed to help people deal with their real guilt. No one could be naïve enough to deny this. However, to deny the possibility of neurotic guilt seems equally naïve. To deny that there are persons whose feeling of guilt is vastly exaggerated or attached to things of no moral significance whatsoever is naïve and destructive.

When Mowrer makes such a claim, he is bound to base it on some presuppositions. One essential presupposition is a solid " code of ethics." If the minister is going to be treating mental illness in terms of real guilt as a source, he must have some universally acceptable code against which to measure the depth of his counselee's involvement in guilt. But no universally accepted code exists. Real ethics belong to the field of dynamic and not of static codes. When the parishioner sees ethics as a code and feels a burden of guilt, the minister's problem may be complex but his opportunity is obvious.

If the guilt is neurotic guilt, it should be handled by a professional who is trained in psychoanalytic psychotherapy. If it is real guilt, then the task belongs logically to the minister. He frequently must deal with the problem of real guilt on the part of real persons. Then he is faced with the problem of helping persons to be released from their burden. The confessional is frequently thought of as an appropriate tool. But the degree of authority that is vested in the church and in the minister is limited. Even in the Roman Catholic Church, where the confessional and the sacrament are more widely used, it is doubtful that everyone is really helped in dealing with guilt through these means. Even so, auricular confession is perhaps one of the most effective tools available to the church. This type of confession is available to the Protestant minister, although not in the formal sense. He has opportunity to listen to his parishioner make confession. The actual spelling out of the acts can be therapeutic. The authority that goes with the image of the minister can be used to help set the person's conscience at ease if this is appropriate.

He may also be able to encourage the use of other methods which are perhaps helpful in dealing with guilt. This would seem to be an appropriate use of his image of authority. One of these is the exercise of a neglected element in the sacrament of penance. It is restitution — restitution for the wrong that has been committed frequently can help to set guilty feelings at rest. A man who has stolen property is likely to continue to feel guilty so long as he retains possession of the stolen goods. If he lets go of it and returns it to its rightful owner, he has increased the possibility of sensing real forgiveness. Restitution is an unpopular idea, but it is also one of the more fruitful spiritual disciplines.

The sense of forgiveness that seems to elude so many people in the Protestant discipline can be nurtured by careful use of the public confessional. Any worship should include a public confession, and it is appropriate for the public confession to be followed by a period of meditation. It is possible for persons to be guided in the use of this period. If they can be helped beforehand so that this period of meditation can be used in such a way that they can be silently specific about their own sins, they may find release. The minister's role here is to offer guidance in the use of this public worship.

The actual substance of a great deal of the guilt expressed to the minister seems to be guilt over finitude. The person comes with the complaint that he cannot feel the presence of God. Sometimes he will speak of having committed the "unpardonable sin," or will complain that he cannot pray as he ought. These are really confessions to a finite nature. The only antidote to this sense of guilt is a direct statement of the worth of the person making the confession (although it is not expected that a man be this unsubtle). But if a minister has any authority, he should certainly use it appropriately to affirm the worth of the person with whom he has to do. When a sense of sin and guilt burden any person, God's grace has preceded that sin. We are already forgiven. The pastor can bring *this* fact of God's love to bear and he should do so.

But this is not always able to release persons from guilt. There is often a deep psychological block that must be dealt with on the level of feeling. Such a feeling-level treatment of guilt is suggested by Fritz Kunkel.[4] It is called "confessional meditation." If you have wronged someone or if you are overcome by anger at another person because of what he has done to you — then take that person before God. Make confession of your own anger. Tell God how unjustly you have been treated and, if you can do so — in the presence of God — curse that person in your imagination. This becomes a real self-exposure before God. It is a subjective way of dealing with both anger and guilt, and it can be a releasing experience.

This method of confession is one that is thoroughly consistent with the pastor's image, in most cases. He frequently has authority sufficient to commend such an exercise. There is good Biblical ground for confessional meditation. The cursing psalms and the curse section of Ps. 139 all indicate that Judeo-Christian tradition demands this earthy attitude toward feeling. The intimate relation between anger and a sense of guilt means that in many situations they must be dealt with together. This is what Kunkel suggests. When guilt is deeply *felt*, there is good reason to believe that it is directly related to anger and a technique such as he suggests may be releasing.

The minister has no mystical authority in the Protestant tradition with which to forgive guilt. He does, however, even in the Protestant cultus, have authority that makes it possible for him to commend to persons means by which they can achieve some freedom. It is appropriate that the minister use this authority to guide people into a more satisfying life.

Dealing with Mental Illness

No pastor escapes the necessity of dealing with persons who have suffered with mental or emotional illness. Frequently, the problem comes to him late. This may happen because his position represents status to the family. They may not want to lose face with this level of society and they may try to keep knowledge of the situation from him.

It is terribly important that a pastor keep communication

open between himself and the families of his parish. The problem of status, that is, a certain degree of social prestige, attaching to the minister is more prevalent in the eastern part of the United States than in the western. There is little or no real social distinction for the clergy in the western part of the United States. Yet, it is truly a great help to have the general public regard the minister as less prestigious than other professionals. Mental illness is still stigmatized in many places, and this barrier between family and minister can be somewhat set aside if the minister does not represent status.

In cases where the pastor has been called into the situation late, he may visit with the patient in a mental hospital. It is useful for a minister to make himself well acquainted with hospital facilities, procedure, and legal arrangements surrounding those procedures. He should be familiar with the laws governing the status of the mentally ill. If state laws provide that mentally ill persons are committed by the courts upon petition by families or others, the minister should be well aware of the particular position of the patient he visits. Has this person been committed by the court? Is the individual a ward of the court or is he here by choice? These are important questions, and the minister should know the answers to them. The answers will indicate to whom the minister is primarily responsible. Of course, his first concern is with the patient. A pastor is nearly always allowed to visit the patient in a mental hospital. At times, he is the only outsider allowed. Frequently, the family of the patient are deeply involved in the dynamic of his illness and this limits or eliminates a good deal of their usefulness as visitors. Usually the hospital staff is too small to give much attention to individual patients. It will often be the case that the minister is the one who has the greatest opportunity to be of real help.

The minister's image may produce a violent reaction in some patients. He may find that he elicits a violent response from the patient simply because he is a minister. His role can cause the patient to be confused. The outward manifestations of mental illness are often couched in religious symbolism. A person with paranoid delusions may identify with God, with Christ, or with Joan of Arc. The force of this syndrome is often emphasized by the clergyman. In this case, it is a difficult thing to withdraw from the situation and abdicate the role, but if such a violent reaction takes place, the minister might logically withdraw. There may be some situations that are so highly charged with negative feeling that there is no creative use of the minister's image possible.

One of the simple but important opportunities afforded to the minister in relation to the mentally ill is that of helping the patient with reality orientation. Many people are terribly afraid of mental patients. Some are anxious because they feel that it is necessary to humor the patient. Such persons often believe that when a patient has paranoid delusions (if he feels that people are out to get him or if he hears voices), his opinion should be tolerated or even reinforced. This is not the case. The patient often needs reality orientation. He may need to have someone be gently firm about the fact that these are delusions. In the case of some persons whose paranoid symptoms are mild, or are not set, there is the possibility of a great deal of help. A quiet insistence on reality can be very important. If a person believes that he smells bad, it is not appropriate to reinforce this delusion. At the same time, it is not helpful to attack the patient's own delusional system directly. It is not necessary to say, " No, you don't smell bad," or, " No, it's all in your head," or, " That is only a delusion on your part." It is more useful and less threatening for the minister to refer to his own experience of reality. " I do not smell anything unpleasant," or, " I have an acute sense of smell, but I cannot notice any odor."

In this way, the minister may be able to help the person deal with his paranoid symptom by reference to his understanding of reality with no attack whatsoever on the patient or his understanding of reality. In a situation such as that described above, the authority of the minister can have real and positive value. The patient may trust the clergyman's word more than the doctor's or the nurse's or more than his family's. I have seen this happen when a rather severely paranoid person came home from the therapist to our home. He would be safe at " the Reverend's house," he believed.

If the clergyman uses his authority in this case, he should do so with great care. He may be the one stable point on the horizon of the patient. It is important that he remain a stable point. It is important that he not destroy the communication between them. There was a time in our society when there were a lot of stable points. The members of the community had a particular category into which the members of the family all fitted. Their actions were predictable, and it was possible to be oriented to the community and to know who you were yourself because others had definite positions in the total spectrum. This is no longer the case. It is frequently one of the tragic facts of life for the inner world of the mentally ill. One of the last remaining points of reference may be the minister. He may not relish this position and he may be subject to constant irritating misunderstanding, but it also may be one of the most important contributions he can make.

More and more the helping professions that work with the mentally ill are turning to the subject of meaning. What is it which gives meaning to life? It is the *anomie* and the vacancy of life which puts such a tax on persons that they fall into depressions. It is necessary to give these persons a new sense of reality and meaning in that reality.

It is quite natural for people to look to the church for meaning. When they turn to the clergyman, he has a unique opportunity to turn his role and image into something of use to the patient. He is expected to demonstrate meaning and to bear witness to the fact of that meaning. Sometimes life closes in on us all. When it closes in to the degree that meaning is lacking, then there is an opportunity for the pastor to speak out a word of meaning.

Now, there are situations in which the pastor will have a

sense of the absurdity of life instead of a sense of meaning. His own subjective life and the pain that he witnesses and feels may make him cry out in curses to God. It is even within the realm of possibility that when he sees someone whom he loves in a state of painful mental illness, he may ask in his own viscera the profound questions of life. What is the meaning and purpose of all this pain? But here again, he is not to be bound by his feelings. He is required to be a professional and to bear witness whether his feelings conform to the witness or not. His own subjective feelings are not the barometer of truth. It is his professional responsibility to bear proper witness no matter how he feels.

Dealing with Family Crises

If he is a pastor of a congregation, one of the most unique qualities of the minister's position is the constant contact that he is allowed at all levels of family life. He has a relationship with a few special families, all of whose members are related to the church in some way. In other situations, he has a relationship with one or more members of a family constellation through the church. This means that he has a very special chance to relate to that total family. This is an opportunity not allowed to other professionals except in rare cases.

If the pastor knows something about group dynamics and about the way people relate to each other in groups, he may be an invaluable counselor to each member in turn. If he is simply regarded as a family friend, he has a chance to observe, to relate, and often to help the whole group toward maturity.

As one related to the family, the minister is drawn into the high points of life and into the valleys of despair. In a long pastorate, he may find that he is able to baptize the children, marry some of the young people, bury the grandparents, and in the course of the years be called upon to counsel the lovesick, encourage the frustrated parent, look for the teen-ager in the wee hours of the night, and perhaps make significant hospital calls once a year. All this in one family complex. There are some who would call this sentimental, but it is the lifeblood of the pastorate. This is the sort of human contact with persons which keeps a man alive.

His experience in family relationship frequently begins in the counseling of those about to be married. In this setting, he has a unique opportunity as a minister. The couple who come to his study are frequently filled with the sort of mutual acceptance and love that gives them a special openness. Along with this warmth, there is also anxiety and ambivalence present in the couple. They have probably wondered privately about what they are doing. They have wondered about what the consequences of this change in status will be. Neither of them has ever seen the other in the married state. They do not know whether this person, who looks so reliable now, will continue to be reliable after marriage.

If the pastor wishes to open this anxiety so that all may look at it, he has only to mention the subject. Other professions do not offer this opportunity. Frequently, the minister is the only one with whom this couple will talk seriously before marriage. They may go to the doctor for a physical examination. If they do, they will go separately and much of the conversation will be about contraceptives or health. Only with the clergyman do they expect any conversation about the real meaning of the event of marriage.

It is an easy subject to open. All that is needed is the question, " How do you know that Mary is reliable and will not deliberately hurt you? " or, " What evidence do you have that John will not desert you after six months? " These questions may startle and shock a couple, but they are legitimately the area for the pastor to discuss. They may be surprised that he has actually touched this depth of concern, but he is not likely to be resented. One of the peculiar qualities of his image is that this is an area in which he very obviously belongs.

The minister is thought of as the representative of " faith."

The church is the community of faith. Faith is the essential ingredient of the marriage relationship. This may not be verbalized but it is deeply sensed by people who stand on the verge of marriage. They know that they enter a dangerous and unknown territory in marriage and they know basically that they do so as an act of faith.

There are some ministers who resent the couple who come to the church to be married after having neglected the Christian community for a long time. This resentment is not justified. If they are asked why they wish to be married in the church, they will say, " I want my marriage to be something special," or, "We want to remember this as a spiritual occasion." The fact is that the more thoughtful persons turn to the church for some support in the marriage relationship. They know that there is risk in the relationship and they frequently express a sense of need for the support of the community in Christ.

Every relationship of life is risky. Every time we extend our love or our concern to another person we take the risk of being rejected and hurt. This is supremely true in marriage. Of course, we can regulate, to some degree, the extent of the risk that we take in marriage. People can have their relationships at various levels. But all relationships that involve risk to our person demand acts of faith. We know that this is the case. If the minister listens carefully, he will hear people who are on the verge of marriage speak in these terms. They may use a nontheological language, but the conversation reveals the same categories of faith-risk-restoration which are the essence of the good news of resurrection. The act of faith that is taken by a couple in marriage is essentially similar to the fundamental act of faith that we associate with belief in God. An act of faith is an act of faith. There is no such thing as one act of faith in God and another act of faith toward persons. Both are the same thing.

A man may state his faith in God and, by the public confession of that faith, unite with the Christian community in the church. This can be the end of the matter. He may, henceforth, make no decision whatsoever on the basis of the faith he has confessed. This is not frequently the case, but theoretically, it could be the case. Faith is always prior to decision. And most of us, even those who have made some confession of faith in God, live as agnostics. Some live with a suspicion that God is — that God is personal — that God is love. Occasionally, we allow this faith to influence the way in which we make up our minds about real things.

For example, a man who believes that God is love should make up his mind according to this precept. If he must make a choice in business between that which is loving and that which is profitable, he should decide on the side of his "belief in God." That is, he should choose the loving decision. Our decisions are not always, perhaps not often, influenced by our belief. Yet no belief that does not influence decision is worthy of the name "faith."

It is this deeper kind of faith which is capable of influencing decision that forms the core of adequate marriage. The total marriage is " one fleshness." Few, however, come even close to this relationship. We take risks in our self-exposure in marriage according to our faith in the other person. If a man believes in the girl he marries in the sense of faith ("the assurance of things hoped for, the conviction of things not seen," Heb. 11:1), then he will risk every part of his person in the relationship. That is, he will dare to be truthful, open, and honest with his spouse. The same is true in the other direction.

Perhaps this is too ideal. Essentially, a couple can be thoroughly married on a less profound level than this total commitment. But they should be aware of the limited nature of their relationship. Marriage is a state of vulnerability. This is what makes it an act of faith or a continuing series of acts of faith. It is this vulnerability that gives real meaning and depth to the sexual relationships of marriage. Sex outside of marriage is shallow and superficial because the persons engaged in the act can so easily disengage themselves. Their whole person need not be involved in the act because no responsibility is exchanged. Such sex is far safer. One will feel less pain, but the meaning goes out of sex at the same time the risk goes out of it.

Every time a relationship is broken, it requires an act of faith to restore the relationship. Suppose John comes home feeling cross and grumpy. He finds Mary in the kitchen, equally frayed and irritated. The two of them have words over anything in particular, and he stomps out of the kitchen in a huff. He sits down rumpling the evening paper and swearing under his breath. She begins to do the dishes a little more vigorously.

Someone in this situation must perform an act of faith. Mary must dry her hands, go into the living room, sit down and begin the approach, "John, let's talk this over again." In doing this, she takes a real risk. She risks his rejection again and the pain which goes with this rejection. She takes this risk because she believes the relationship can be resurrected. She believes that the possible pain of her rejection is worth the risk because the relationship can be raised to a new value. If she does not take this risk and he refuses to take it, the relationship will remain in its broken state.

Faith is faith. Faith in God is expressed in faith reactions toward persons. A resurrection faith is expressed in the willingness to enter into real relationships with others.

None of this sort of depth is ordinarily touched by the non-minister. Yet, the minister is *expected* to speak in these terms. This is a unique opportunity which is afforded him. It is important not to be drawn into philosophy or theology that is not related to life. Probably the least fruitful of all conversations is the one which is completely theological and makes no application of that theology to life. The minister is in the midst of life as he counsels with a couple about to be married. He has a ready-made situation into which theology can be injected and its implication made directly. This is truly unique.

There are other family situations that have fruitful possibilities. At the time of the baptism of children, the parents expect some conversation with the pastor. He is able to discuss the many facets of the risky, painful, joyful business of parenthood with those parents. It is an opening into real and vital areas of life that is not available to anyone except the pastor. It should be honored by use.

In relating to the family, the pastor carries a particular image. It is not always positive but it has always been conditioned by the attitudes of the parents, the grandparents, and the aunts and uncles. Yet the image has overtones of expectation that can be used.

How do we meet the image in relation to the family and use it? First, the pastor is expected to be close to the family. He is often trusted in the family complex. Secondly, he is called into the family at crisis points. He is called at high festivals and deep depressions. He should remain open to approach. It is not good judgment to be forever asking questions or probing into family business. But when the time comes that he is needed and the need for him is established in the minds of family members, he can be called.

Ministry to the Alienated

The pastor is called into relation to lonely people more eagerly than he may wish to be called. The rejected or confused ones who live on the fringes of social groups are still approachable by the pastor. Frequently, they will approach him because he is the one who is open in society. In a ministry to this particular segment of his parish the pastor has unique opportunities. First of all, if he is minister of a parish, he has the opportunity to manipulate deliberately the development of relationships among people of his parish. He can suggest that the Joneses have the Smiths over for dinner. It is even within his power, at some time, deliberately to see that the Smiths have the Joneses for dinner. In a society as loosely knit as ours, no one should make apology for a manipulation of people if it gets them into valid and fruitful contact with one another. My personal attitude is deeply colored by the fact that two of the parishes I have served have been in highly mobile communities. In these communities, if you are going to have any social interlacing at all, it must be established quickly. And this frequently calls for some kind of manipulation.

In a mobile megalopolis, two groups of persons are particularly prominent. First, the young unmarried adults who flow past, and the young married people who move as soon as they raise a down payment for a home in the suburbs. This is the first category. Secondly, there is, in most mobile areas, a layer of the older community. These are the men and women who may have originally lived in the community before it came in for extensive development. The pastor has a responsibility to both of these groups. They both deserve a ministry and must be approached in completely different ways because of the differing images they hold of the clergy and because of the variety of their needs. How does the minister approach the older parishioner and how does he use positive aspects of his image with this older group? He should be cautious so as not to damage the personal relationship by confusing reaction to the image they may have placed upon him. At the same time, he must relate to other age groups and he dare not assume the role placed upon him by the senior citizens. This will cut him off from any meaningful conversation with them at all. The minister will feel division at this point. Confusion and pain are inevitable. There may be, even worse, a feeling of hypocrisy. He may feel that his position lacks integrity. But if the role he assumes is best for the lonely person who needs his ministry, he should reconcile himself to irritation. It is part of his professional responsibility to maintain meaningful contact with different segments of society. This does not mean that he has lost his identity. It means that he is attempting to use his role creatively.

The group of rootless and lonely young people is an important area. Here the minister has a special opportunity and responsibility. He can work to establish a welcoming warmth within the church he serves so that this segment of the community is encouraged to relate to that church. He has other more personal opportunities for ministry also. This group is not only more open and questioning but has a lot of other characteristics. Most often they are lonely. Frequently they are alienated. The young unmarried of a mobile community are active and frequently not aware that they are lonely and alienated.

A church and a pastor have a special type of ministry in a community of lonely young adults. One church has a special way of celebrating the Lord's Supper. This form of the Communion incorporates a feast into the Communion. In brief: the elders prepare a hearty stew on the Saturday before the celebration. This is done by the group in the church kitchen. Then each member of the congregation is asked to bring a loaf of bread to morning worship. These are taken out of the cupboards of their homes or off the shelves of the local grocery. They are brought forward during the service and placed on a table beside the Communion table. At the point in the service where the bread of the Communion is consecrated, the loaves that have been brought from home are included in that blessing. The service is very much as it is on other days but may include a meditation on the meaning of Christian fellowship and the particular significance of the " agape feast " in New Testament times.

The worship is not concluded in the sanctuary. During the hymn of meditation, the elders come forward, take the bread and carry it to the fellowship hall. They are followed by the choir, the pastor, and the congregation. When they arrive on the lower floor, the stew is served by the elders, along with the bread. People are encouraged to talk and visit. Certainly, this is appropriate if this is to be a fellowship feast and it is clearly in keeping with old and honored tradition in the Eastern Orthodox Church. After all have eaten one helping of the stew, along with hearty pieces of the bread, the pastor can give the charge and the benediction. This means that the worship has continued into and through the meal. It has capacity somehow to give a new quality to the fellowship. Especially those who are alone can be deeply blessed by this kind of observance. They can and will linger for prolonged visits after the worship meal has concluded.

In order for the minister to take part in such an observance, he must preserve an adequate relationship to the church and its tradition. It may seem more popular and easier for the pastor to relate to young adults by presenting to them a sophisticated image which is "modern" in every way. But in doing so, he may rob those young people of the opportunity to relate to the tradition of the church or to anything except to the pastor as a person. If the minister is a professional in the best sense, he will not allow this to happen. Granted that the role is not always comfortable, nevertheless it remains filled with opportunities.

Clerical garb is sometimes a useful tool in relating to the lonely. It is possible to go virtually anywhere on useful business if your office is announced by proper garb. It has special uses in a ministry to the lonely. It is an invitation to them to make an approach, and many will do so.

The garb is also a symbol of possible initiative on the part of the minister. The definition of a professional includes the fact that he must be capable of being a self-starter and functioning under his own supervision. This kind of competence should be a part of the capacity of a pastor. Many areas of the community are open to him as a professional, and one of the tragedies is that so few men take advantage of their opportunities. A minister can ring doorbells all over the community and take initiative in a variety of social and political groups. There is a sense in which his effectiveness will increase in direct proportion to the incongruity of his situation at the moment. If he is not expected to call, he may be even more likely to produce some effect from his contact.

A minister can sit all evening in a local bar with no questions asked. If he is open, he will be approached by a great many people. Some of them will have deep troubles which they would like to discuss. It should not be assumed that these people are less confused or hypocritical because they are in a bar instead of in a church. The conversation will probably be no more fruitful than the discussion in a Bible class, but it will probably be just as fruitful. The facts of the case are that the people in saloons are just as wicked or troubled as anyone else. On the negative side, they may have their senses somewhat clouded by alcohol. On the positive side, they are frequently less insulated by the vocabulary and categories of theological language. It is, therefore, sometimes possible to talk with them about real issues. It is somewhat easier to avoid " religious conversation " in a bar than it is in a church meeting. (Not much easier, but a little easier.) Conversation in bars has a limited usefulness, but it does constitute a legitimate use of the role. The objection may be made that this kind of conduct is almost bound to alienate the older people of the church. They may be offended by the pastor's behavior. However, if this exposure of the role is deliberate and purposeful, it can be the basis for useful reinterpretation of the ministry and of the mission of the church.

The minister has gone to the saloon wearing his garb and not incognito. This is important because he will be misunderstood if he goes without this identity. If the pastor has gone deliberately into this particular offending situation, and if he has gone with the purpose of ministry, then he can use the offense as a means of reinterpreting his role as shepherd to all. This is only possible if he really has gone with purpose. That " little old lady " will know if he has gone with purpose or not when he tries to reinterpret his role to her.

There are some reasons for going into the setting of the bar which are not legitimate. One illegitimate reason would be to drink. But this is probably not a frequent reason among ministers. If they have problems along that line, they will probably drink at home. The second inappropriate reason would be curiosity. No one who is there out of morbid curiosity will be admitted to the community of the saloon or the cocktail lounge. Bars, especially neighborhood bars, have a very distinct community in each. The distinction should be made between the neighborhood bar or the established tavern and the cocktail lounge. Cocktail lounges attached to restaurants seldom have the characteristics that are here assigned to saloons. They have a more transient clientele and therefore offer less opportunity for the minister. But in the neighborhood bar, which is frequented by the same group night after night, the people will meet for a drink, visit a few minutes, exchange pleasantries or a joke, renew their sense of belonging, take the sacrament (that is, finish their drink), and depart. There are exceptions to this pattern. "Serious drinkers" are accepted. But for many people in the neighborhood tavern, going to the saloon is very much like going to church. The pastor who feels called upon to enter this kind of ministry should be aware that these communities are closed. It may take a long time to gain admittance to the family. Each bar has its own group even though one person may relate to several groups. The opportunity exists for an uninhibited, serious-minded but noncondemning minister in this setting to be part of the community while not being captured by its philosophy. His job is to bring another witness into this setting.

Jesus began a ministry in the synagogue, but toward the end he was much more concerned with the alienated peoples. Is there some appropriate parallel here which implies that a man can begin his ministry within the church community but after establishing his person in that environment, he should turn to the alienated — "first the lost sheep of Israel," then the world?

If a minister tries this sort of shepherding ministry, he must be careful. It is not appropriate for him to drink very much. Probably he should not be absolutely dry, but he should go heavy on Calso water and on the long, tall, weak drinks. If he cannot learn to nurse a gin and tonic for a long time, he should stay away from alcohol altogether. In the setting of the saloon with his garb on, he ought never to forget that he is working. A second problem is the need to reinterpret this ministry to the total congregation and to the community. The minister is not "going down there to help those poor people." Rather, he is making himself available as a shepherd to people who do not even know he exists. He is exposing himself to opportunities that the church has forgotten about. He is relating to a world which is there whether the church admits it is there or not. But *he is not slumming*. Not everyone will understand this to be the case, no matter how much the pastor may try to interpret. There will be people in the church who don't understand. More important, there will be people in the saloons who do not understand. These are the ones to whom he must interpret his role most carefully. It is terribly important that he be utterly unambiguous about what he is doing. He himself must know what he is about.

When he comes to the matter of interpreting the role to the person he meets in the setting of the local pub, he must not assume that he is accepted as a person. Actually, the most rigid misinterpretations of the role of the minister are in the minds of people who do not know the church. Many of them have rejected the church because of what they understood as a rigid, moralistic, hypocritical character which they saw in religious people. I read about a little girl one time who prayed, "God, please make all the bad people good, and the good people nice."

The local tavern is filled with persons who see the minister with these rigid characteristics. At the same time, many of them regard themselves as "bad." They must be "bad" (they feel) because they hang around the saloon and don't go to church. The role of the minister is critical in this situation. In a sense, he is the key to a new understanding on the part of this person. It is important, desperately important, for the "alienated" to know that the church is a society of sinners, that it is made up of people who are not good and who know that they are not good. By his own carriage and behavior, the minister can begin to plant a new understanding in the minds of those who are separated from the Christian community.

He cannot condemn. He has no base from which to judge another. He has professed a loyalty to and a faith in the validity of the church as a community of believers. When the alienated attack the community of the church, as they will, he is the interpreter. He cannot defend the church as it is. The church cannot be defended as it is. It can only be understood in dynamic terms and in terms of its witness.

He may be able to say, "You feel you have grounds to reject the church. You have no idea what corruption and lack of effectiveness exists in the church. You only get this sort of information from the inside. The minister has more reason to be disillusioned than anyone outside. But the church is still a useful, valid secular tool. I am committed to it." Now, if the alienated one says, "Why?" then let the minister think about it for himself. It will be more exercise than a dozen sermons.

It is inappropriate to generalize, but the impression remains that the alienated are an opinionated group. They may be violently right or violently left, but generally speaking, they have deep prejudices. This should not surprise the minister. After all, he works within the church with prejudiced people all the time. But there ought to be no impression that people in bars are easier to communicate with than people in the church.

The kind of exposure of which I am speaking is not particularly pleasant. But men who serve parishes in the megalopolis know that the confrontation cannot be avoided unless we are willing to settle for complete irrelevance. No one can serve a parish in the midst of a vast sea of persons to whom the church has no relationship and simply forget that they exist. Unless the church meets this kind of challenge through its clergy, it will be relegated to the sidelines of society. It is being forced into a conversation with the world. If the minister is willing to assume his professional responsibility, he will take part in the conversation.

Any attempt at such a ministry should be within the context of deliberate, scientifically evaluated experiment. There is no place for adolescent diddling. The work of relating to this " outside " group will consume great amounts of time and psychic energy. It should be done efficiently.

The problem of talking to those who are outside the sociological context of the church is a threatening thing to the pastor. How does he manage to work up the courage to speak to someone on the " outside " seriously? He is used to talking to believers, since most preaching in the standard-brand church is " pastoral " by the old definition. This means that the smiling faces, nodding heads, or gentle laughter of those friendly saints can prove to be a powerful anodyne. But the minister who steps out of his context into the free-for-all of the great books discussion or the local bar must have: (1) faith in the resurrection — faith that his stumbling can be used creatively by God; (2) willingness to look foolish together with enough humility to study the intellectual categories in which the other man thinks and speaks; (3) a faith that has existential meaning for himself. By this is meant a faith which is directly related to the decision-making process.

Unless a minister has faith that his own foolishness can be raised to life by the Holy Spirit, he will be reluctant to venture into the threats of secular conversation. This does not mean that he is committed by that resurrection faith to look foolish deliberately. The responsibility to learn the new categories of humanity is a part of the professional responsibility of the pastor. The fundamentalist seems to be somehow wedded to the idea that the pastor's looking foolish is the significant and critical tool of the Holy Spirit. Suicide is not the source of resurrection. The man who dies reluctantly for God's purpose is a candidate for resurrection. Jesus' crucifixion has meaning because he went to the cross after Gethsemane, where he prayed that the cup of death might be removed. His death has its ultimate meaning in the wake of his constant attempt to explain himself and teach men. It was the rejection by those whom Jesus had tried desperately to love and to teach which brought him to the cross. He was careful and deliberate in seeking ways to interpret himself to his contemporaries and he used the context of the persons whom he confronted in his attempt to interpret that truth. He did not rush to the cross. He went regretfully, and while he went he tried to teach by being as clear as possible to all men.

For the minister who steps into a threatening new social and intellectual context, this should mean that he too is called to learn new language and use it with sympathy. If he is cut to foolishness after real struggle to understand and communicate, God's Spirit has chance and reason for resurrection because there has been meaningful death or, at least, meaningful and risky investment of life.

This is only possible if the faith of the minister is an existential faith. It must be a faith " in order to " and capable of influencing the decision-making process. If the faith of the minister is at the level of intellectual assent, it is less than " existential " in this sense. If faith is the adjusting of intellectual dials on the unspoken theory that there is somehow merit in this adjustment, then this faith is untranslatable. This is a superstition which dies reluctantly, and by some of those who treasure the church as an ingroup is held with a passionate clasp. The vast capacity of irrelevant theological debate to absorb some of the ingroup is sign of this womb-seeking syndrome. How can the truth or the untruth of a doctrine such as the virgin birth possibly affect the way in which a man makes up his mind on an ethical issue?

A faith that is translatable into decision and action is also portable into another social and intellectual framework. The description of real events and real decisions is translatable. This means that the pastor's faith must be of the quality which influences his life. There is need for every man who tries such an experiment to assess his own capacity to tolerate the frustration and humiliation. He should stay well within his capacity to tolerate the pain of these encounters because he needs a little steam left over for his own use.

It should be noted that motivation is the critical thing. The reinterpretation that is possible in this setting will never take place if the primary motive of the minister is morbid curiosity, thirst, or a passion to reinterpret *himself*. He must have a " professional " concern. This is another way of saying that he must be there as a representative of the church.

All places are open to the clergyman if he is properly garbed — the police station, the emergency ward, the jail, or the mental hospital. He is admitted into all without question, and it is appropriate that he use this freedom for some useful purpose.

The local police, if properly approached, may be willing to call the minister when a juvenile is picked up. They may be especially eager to have help if they can find no one who will assume responsibility for the young person. Before this kind of trust will be placed in a minister, he must establish his own reputation for integrity, for being close-mouthed, and for real concern. Here again, morbid curiosity will not do as a motive. There must be concern for the person involved.

The local hospital may also respond by calling the minister in for emergencies if he will take the trouble to be known by the staff and if he can establish a reputation for concern and integrity. It is the lonely ones of society who need the pastor the worst. It is frequently the lonely one who has rejected him the most firmly because he has misunderstood the image. Nevertheless, it is the image that makes it possible for the pastor to take initiative in reestablishing the contact.

The matter of clerical garb is much debated. It is a great annoyance to some, a shelter to others. Actually, it is a tool. It should be taken up, as a tool, when the job calls for its use. There is no reason to be enslaved by the garb so that one is never without it. This implies that the clergyman is somehow himself the focus of the church, that his very body is involved in some unique way with the church. This would be the danger of the Roman Catholic custom which insists that a priest be identified at all times as a priest. (In a catalog of ecclesiastical goods some years ago, I recall an advertisement for "clerical pajamas." This is a sadly twisted attitude toward clerical garb.)

If the job at hand can be helped forward by the use of the collar, then the collar should be used. As indicated above, it is not safe or proper for a minister to "work" in a saloon without the garb. He may go to a bar on his own when he is "off duty" without the garb. That is his own business. But he should wear his uniform while he is on duty. Doors open for the man in a collar. If there is a legitimate reason for being in the jail, or in the hospital, there is every reason to use the easiest means of admittance. Let him use the collar. If it is useful in relation to the lonely, then use it. If it is a deterrent, set it aside.

Avoidance of Religious Conversation

One of the trickiest exercises for the minister is the avoidance of religious conversation. We have talked about the ministry of a man in the bar or in the church or in the hospital. One of the dangers which is constant is that a minister's conversation will be religious in symbol and language instead of being related directly to life.

Suppose a minister meets a young man in a bar. The young man is made bold by the collar and begins a conversation because it seems to be invited by the garb. He may also be responding negatively to the authority that is represented in the garb or he may be seeking a figure who can help him to "justify himself" in past conduct or in anticipated conduct.

The natural trend of conversation in this context is toward religion. This is the easy place for the young man to lead the conversation. It is a safe area because in our generation one man's opinion about religious matters is regarded as of equal validity with all other opinions. Besides, religion as a subject deals in the field of generalities. In this lovely field, it is possible to pick the little flowers of justification which the young man may wish to gather. (It is interesting that two widely read treatments of ethics in recent years — Cox's *The Secular City* and Fletcher's *Situation Ethics* — touch only slightly upon the subject of sex. Yet they are widely quoted in this area. They are quoted with the shallowest understanding and, for the most part, in order to justify behavior that is not condoned by either author. This is one of the dangers of generality.)

Religious conversation has the danger of all generalized conversation. It can be readily misinterpreted. This does not mean that such conversation is always bad or useless. It can frequently be used to open deeper and more real conversation about real problems and real decisions. If a minister has an attitude toward his religious faith that clearly makes a connection between faith and decision, he will be able to turn the conversation into more important channels. If he attempts this, he must be prepared to lose his contact. It may be that the person with whom he is talking has no interest in a religion which touches his decision-making process. Not everyone is enthusiastic about such a religious view.

Once, in an Inquirers Class, we were talking about the need for faith in relating to other people. One of the men interrupted to say: " What has this got to do with religion? Religion is concerned with my relationship to God, not my relationship to men! " The class had a great time with the discussion that followed. Not all people would be this candid, but an attitude which encourages the separation of decision from faith is found everywhere. It is one of our principal defenses against involvement in God's purpose.

The opening conversation may very well be religious. The temptation of the minister is to remain in his role with the familiar symbols. It is much more difficult to discuss real things and real decisions. The minister can, however, influence the direction of the conversation toward reality. When he does this, he will increase the anxiety level in others and probably in himself because the answers to real questions are always more difficult and far more probing than theoretical answers. If the pastor is working in a bar or at a cocktail party or at a diner and comes upon a real issue, he may be well advised to make whatever contribution he can make to the situation in that moment. The possibility of seeing this same person in another setting at a later time is remote.

If the conversation remains at a religious level, due to anxiety on the part of the other person, the minister may be up against the necessity of reinterpreting his own role before any real communication can take place. Many people respond negatively toward the authority implied in the minister's role, and to put such a person at ease may be essential. How do you do this? This is a complicated question.

As long as the conversation remains on a religious level, it is not possible to solve the question of authority. If the talk can move to the reality level, the authority figure will be put into perspective. The pastor may be flexible on theoretical levels and give no impression except that of weakness. When he enters the reality situation honestly and attempts to speak to the real issue, he will be exposed as a human being. Sometimes, to his own surprise, he will be exposed. But almost always this exposure is for the good of the correspondent. It offers opportunity for reinterpretation.

Dealing with Terminal Illness

One of the really unique places in which the pastor can make use of his role is in dealing with terminal illness. He is welcomed at the bedside of the dying and has the opportunity and the responsibility to witness to the resurrection in this critical setting. He can be related to the physician, the family, and the dying person. He has more opportunity to relate meaningfully to the patient than anyone else because he represents the church, the community of faith, and eternal values. He may not feel that he represents all these things, but in the mind of the dying one, he is the closest of anyone to all these concepts.

The physician has a different role. At the point where illness is called terminal, his authority is no longer applicable. He is in a position to help relieve pain and discomfort. He no longer has any long-term role. The ministry to the dying is one that demands careful appraisal of each situation, and the role of the minister may be completely different in the eyes of different people.

Suppose the pastor is called to the local hospital nursery to baptize the dying child of a family he has never met. He may believe with all his soul that the baptism is not necessary and that God cares for the child equally whether the child has been baptized or not. He may be committed to the view that the community and the parents are essential ingredients in the baptism of infants. He may even feel that to proceed with the baptism puts his own integrity in question. But this is a ministry to the dying. Is it appropriate to interpret all this to the parents or is it more kind and " Christian " to proceed to baptize the child and leave the interpretation till later? Obviously, this latter is what he should do. Dealing with prejudice or superstition in the midst of emotional strain of the kind felt by parents in such a situation is useless and destructive. In a case such as this, the minister is bound by his professional responsibility to use his role rather than be diverted by the desire to interpret his role.

The concept of infant baptism as developed in the Reformed Church centered in the mutual concern of the church family for all covenant children of the church. In a society that is as fluid as that of the United States in the sixties, there is doubt that infant baptism should be retained as a sacrament. But you do not discuss this with the distraught parents of a dying child.

For the young mother who is dying of cancer, there must be a different ministry. Here circumstances should determine the role interpreted by the pastor. If the young woman comes from a background that was steeped in Bible and church tradition, then she should have a chance to hear the proper words from her pastor. The deathbed is no place to reinterpret a religious faith, and the pastor should be " all things to all men." Now the proper words may be common to both patient and pastor. Appropriate prayers, selections from the Bible, and particularly from the psalms belong in this setting. They do not need to be interpreted in any way that does anything other than give comfort. Certainly, there is possibility that enough creative imagination on the pastor's part will make it possible for him to convey comfort to the dying person. This does not mean that he says things he does not mean. It may be that he will leave unsaid some of the things he would ordinarily say to interpret either Biblical material or his role. He may have reservations about certain types of public verbal prayer. But he does not talk about the doubts. If he is a real professional, he does what is expected of him. Out of a concern for the person for whom he has responsibility, he will assume the role that is most helpful in the moment.

Ministry to an older person who is dying can also demand imagination. Those who were raised a generation ago often have mental images of the minister which seem to be much more stable than those which prevail now. Their image may be one of authority and " old-fashioned " conviction which is quite foreign to our day. Does this mean that these people must be left without a ministry that seems appropriate to them? Granted that they need to have the same startling jars that all others have when they are well enough to fight back. But when they are dying, it seems right to let them see the image they wish to see or need to see. With proper imagination and ingenuity, the pastor should be able to find the words to say and the stance to assume that will be most helpful. The role does not need to be interpreted in the moment. It is the minister who suffers from the incongruity of the situation. It is appropriate for the servant to suffer. It is the least he can do for those who are dying.

The physician may need a ministry as well. He is suffering from the pain of having done his best to save life and failed. He is not trained to speak to the needs of the patient or the family in this situation. He may have learned a great deal from experience but he is not trained for this role. If he finds a minister whom he can trust, he will call that man to help in the critical moment. It is surprising that there is not a closer working relationship between physicians and ministers. They seem so essential to each other. One is tempted to say that it may be a combination of busyness on the part of the physician and semiprofessional conduct and busybodiness on the part of some ministers which keeps this cooperation limited.

The physician can minister to the pastor. Long, wee-hour conversations with physicians have been among the high points of my ministry. The problem of pain is troublesome to both physician and minister. The facts about pain, its progress, its level, the meaning of pain threshold — all these need the professional interpretation of the physician. The interpreter of these things can be profoundly helpful to the minister.

James Knight has written some extremely helpful suggestions on the ministry to the terminal patient.[5] There is often a lack of communication between physician and pastor. The physician ordinarily determines the amount of information to be given to the patient as to his condition. There are many times in dealing with terminal patients when information about this matter is not shared with the pastor. When a minister is not aware of the state of the illness, he may find it an advantage. The pastor is expected to be truthful, and it may not be entirely bad for him to be genuinely in the same position as the patient. If he has related to the patient with sufficient human warmth, he may find that the patient may share important information or deep feelings with him. If he knows more than the patient and is restricted from being candid with the patient, this can become a real barrier to his ministry.

The reason for the minister's having information about the

illness may be a valid desire to help, or simply a morbid curiosity. As a general rule, he will be better off if he knows only what the patient shares with him.

The physician may need the ministry of the pastor as much as the patient needs it. For one thing, a physician must make the decision continually as to the proper measures to be taken in order to preserve life. This presents him with a series of extremely difficult questions. They are ethical questions and the physician can never escape them. Modern medical techniques make it possible to prolong life for a long time past the point where such prolongation has any real usefulness. For a person to be surrounded by equipment upon which he depends for life or to have tubes in every orifice of his body is not dignified. If it is too late for the kind of preventive medicine that can give opportunity for meaningful life, then it may be time to cease the heroic last-ditch fight and allow the patient to die in dignity. No patient should be allowed to suffer the agony of dehydration, and intravenous fluid is not necessarily a heroic measure designed to prolong life. It may simply be essential to the patient's comfort. But really extreme measures may have a termination point that favors kindness. In any case, the physician is the custodian of this decision. He is ruled in part by the family, and the family of the patient may be driven by guilt or fear. He may be ill advised to cease treatment in a manner that is too obvious. But he must decide what is to be done.

When a patient can decide for himself the treatment to which he will submit, there may be a value in the thoughtful counsel of a pastor. The pain, discomfort, and expense of cobalt treatments may be rejected because they do not purchase enough time. The family that can be open enough at this point to share in the evaluation of such treatment is very fortunate. The pastor's role may be prayer with and for the patient and his family. He should also encourage them to make a deliberately intelligent decision.

It is difficult to relate to the dying. It is such a vivid reminder of our own finite nature that the pastor may have to force himself into the relationship. He should be aware of his own fear and his own lack of faith when he enters this ultimate area of ministry. He should be more concerned if he feels no fear because this may mean that his facade is too secure. Too great a degree of involvement may crush his spirit. Too little may destroy his usefulness. He is again called upon for professional calculation.

Ministry to the family comes second only to ministry to the dying person. They have need of comfort. Their comfort is more pronounced when the dying person is properly cared for. If the minister is not comfortable in the role, it does not mean that he must spend a major part of his time correcting misunderstandings. He can carry the weight of his role with professional competence and it is appropriate that he should do so. When opportunity arises, he can work to correct that image. But among the dying and those who stand beside them, he must simply carry his role.

A Ministry to the Homosexual

It is possible to maintain a direct and useful contact with members of the homosexual community by simple acceptance of them as persons. Many ministers have unusual opportunities to relate to homosexuals because ministers seem less threatening. It may be that the clergyman's image is somewhat less intense sexually than the image of other persons. (There are, of course, a percentage of homosexuals who enter the ministry. Very few of these are practicing homosexuals in the sense that they act out their drives regularly, or live with persons of the same sex as a couple.) The minister's role seems to imply a certain openness.

A ministry to homosexuals is a part of every clergyman's responsibility and with very few exceptions, I am sure, a part of his parish responsibility. He may be unaware of this fact. If he is unaware, he is naïve.

It is important to make peace with one fact. Many ministers say, "I will tolerate the homosexual as long as he is in treatment looking for some help with his problem." This is not fair or useful. In many communities there exist colonies of practicing homosexuals who have no intention of changing their way of life. They look upon that way of life as valid and preferable to any other way of life. Is the minister ready to deny any ministry to these persons? When they are cut, they bleed. The same problems come upon them that come upon all other members of society. They feel the same pains. Why should they be left without a ministry? Is their sin of "separation" any more odious in the eyes of God than those sins which are part of the regular life of the church family? It is my own opinion that no minister is justified in turning his back upon anyone, no matter what his problem may be. Certainly, he is not justified in turning his back upon the homosexual.

The homosexual community is filled with persons who are interested in the creative arts. This does not mean that homosexuals are a personality type. It is a community of wide diversity. Nevertheless, many of them have an artistic bent. The average minister may have an interest and appreciation along this line which many people do not have. And this sometimes gives a line of communication between minister and homosexual which is unique.

One of the continuing problems of the homosexual is that he is vulnerable. The employers of homosexuals frequently take advantage of this vulnerable state, and so homosexuals are actually one of the persecuted minorities in our society.

Many homosexuals are disturbed by their way of life and some are looking for help in finding a way out. Those who are outwardly content are not always content on a deeper unconscious level. The image of the minister as moral authority is threatening to anyone. The practicing homosexual who is known to the pastor can get some indication from the pastor's reaction as to how well he is accepted. If he is unknown to the pastor, he must judge on the basis of the minister's reactions to other situations and thus discover if the minister can be trusted.

The community of homosexuals gives the impression to an outsider of being a close-knit group. One would expect communication to go through this group very readily. This is not necessarily the case, because the homosexual community is stratified socially. This is especially true in areas where the community is well established and not threatened by outsiders. This means that it becomes larger and is not obliged to be interdependent in the same way as when there is active pressure.

It is a good thing for the minister to be as aware as possible of this group in his town or neighborhood or congregation. Most practicing homosexuals are sophisticated enough to keep to themselves and out of any difficulty with the police. However, in cases where a homosexual does run into problems with the police, he is in need of the same sympathetic, nonjudgmental help that a man in a ministry owes to anyone. No minister should refuse to help in cases of this sort, and yet it is a difficult thing for him to help consistently without being labeled himself.

Although there is no personality type, there are characteristic patterns. When homosexuals are put into positions of leadership, they sometimes carry the dynamic of their outside relationships into the organization where they happen to be leaders. When this takes place, it can become extremely complex, because the dynamic of the outside relationship of the homosexual is hidden. It may not be possible to have the homosexual in places of leadership without the proper checks.

Bergler notes a characteristic pattern in the homosexual.[6] He calls this pattern " injustice gathering " and characterizes it as a tendency to save up injustices suffered in a sort of hoard, spilling them off in one rejection. Bergler suspects that this is the reason for the fact that most homosexual " marriages " or liaisons last only a short time. The pattern of " injustice gathering " can be noted in some homosexuals and is probably a principal reason why they seem ill suited for heavy responsibility in an organization. Many of the homosexual organizations have great difficulty with internal political maneuvering and with the jealousies that arise within the organization.

The Lesbian community is far less available to the male clergyman than that of the male homosexual. It is possible to make some useful contact with this group through mutual friends among the homosexuals. There is some communication between the two groups, especially when they share the same local bars. In a megalopolis in which a great many young women congregate to look for work and excitement, there are many who find nothing else. Although they harbor a nesting instinct, a variety of unhappy love affairs will sometimes be followed by an experience with one of the members of the Lesbian community. They may have a roommate of that persuasion or a close friendship.

At the age of about thirty, these women tend to enter a period of crisis. They sense that they are losing the race for a man and are losing the attraction they once possessed. There is a "thirty-year syndrome" which is not at all rare. A psychotic break may follow upon the depression that results from the sense of loss. Doors have been closed that were formerly opened. Opportunities for mature male companionship are slipping away.

Women caught in this situation are seldom confirmed Lesbians. The sexual experience that they may have had in that context tends, however, to complicate the problem. A great deal of self-doubt can result. This is particularly the case where a girl has had a strict or puritanical background. In this situation the minister has two responsibilities. One is to try to bring a resurrection theology to bear upon the depression. His task is to help revive the hope for a normal life. The second responsibility is to bring the girl to the point where she can get appropriate therapy. At times he may use his position as an authority figure to help at this juncture. From my own experience, I would feel that he ought not to assume the role of therapist in the situation. Rather, he should assume the role of the supportive pastor.

The role of the minister seems to be particularly capable of touching the homosexuals of society. If a pastor can use good judgment in this ministry and not allow it to become a dominant characteristic of his work, he can do a useful work among homosexuals. He ought not to minister to them as a special group. Simply being available as a pastor to these men and women as he is to other persons seems the appropriate thing to do.

There may be a temptation on the part of a clergyman to make use of a special work with homosexuals as a source of publicity. This is not a good idea. In addition to the fact that it adds another complexity to his already difficult task of interpreting his role, it will cut off his usefulness to the homosexual community he hopes to serve. If he is going to be properly "professional," he must use the aspects of his role that are useful, and not add confusion.

Dealing with the Administrative Task

Ministers who are asked to express their opinion place the lowest estimate of interest and importance in the administrative work of the church. This is a bad estimate. Actually, administration comes high on the list of potentially useful aspects of the role of the minister. The administrative work of the church puts the pastor into close, meaningful contact with a large number of people. The process of making real decisions and working with committees who work out the decisions offers a chance to be involved in real dynamics. Working with a body of elders offers opportunity to participate in existential decisions and evaluate those administrative decisions on the base of a dynamic Christian ethic.

The man who considers his ministry to be concerned with "spiritual" matters may have lost his most important means of identity with his laymen. Paul was a tentmaker and was able to understand the world of business because of this fact. The pastor is administrator of a secular organization. This is his best opportunity to know life from the "secular" view.

There are times and places where he is not welcomed into identity with the world. Many laymen wish their pastor to be concerned with what is "Biblical" and "spiritual" and "aesthetic" and "irrelevant." There are pastors of large churches who are freed of all administrative responsibility in order that they may preach. These men may be popular preachers but it is possible that they are not the most useful preachers. There is much complaint about the separation between pulpit and pew. It would be less than honest to deny a certain amount of satisfaction and pleasure in the isolation which is effected by this separation. Neither the pastor nor the parishioner may be eager to have real mutual involvement.

Administration is particularly distasteful to the minister because he has no training in it. He does not feel secure or at home in administration. The seminaries are sadly lacking at this point. Even some seminaries that make a great deal of the necessity to identify with the world and the secular nature of all life are sadly negligent here. What a man learns about administration in the present structure of the church he must pick up as he goes along. Usually he learns nothing about it until he gets out into the parish. After he is out, he may find that the administrative work of the parish is the most difficult part of his job because he knows least about it. Other phases of his work give satisfaction. Administration breeds bitterness, and he ends by finding one of the prime opportunities of his task to be distasteful. Frequently, he goes back to graduate school as an escape and occasionally he leaves the ministry altogether.

If the church is a secular arm, then it is important to teach its leaders efficiency in the work to which they must set their hand. Why this is neglected by the professional school is a real mystery. One of the ways in which a minister has a chance to learn something about the life of the man who works hard in the secular world is to join him. It is not unreasonable to believe that the minister can achieve this identification through his proper function as administrator. A part of his professional responsibility is to keep the machine oiled and going. The sooner he stops bellyaching and learns how to run the machine efficiently, the sooner he will have a chance to be useful in his human contacts. The more efficiently his unavoidable administration is cared for the more time he will have for study.

One of the constant complaints of pastors when they get together is concern with the excessive demands made upon them. They will complain at length about the long hours of work, the time-consuming confusion of meetings, and the lack of consideration from the people of the parish. This sort of "Monday morning talk" is probably out of all proportion to the facts.

The owner of a small business with a half dozen employees will spend much more time at his work than the average pastor spends at his. In addition, he will often spend that time in one place. Frequently, he will spend it doing bookkeeping for the Internal Revenue Service until late at night. He will do this work for a purpose which seems less important than the work of the ministry. Possibly he will complain. Frequently, the owner of a small business does complain. The medical doctor and the dentist complain. But the minister not only complains; he often rejects the administrative responsibility as useless busywork. It is not that. It is potentially a great source of teaching and real practice in Christian ethics.

If the minister wanted to work a forty-hour week, he could do so. But having accepted the professional category, he should be reconciled. This does not mean that he must always be happy at being called out at three in the morning by an alcoholic. He does not have to be ecstatic when he has meetings night after night for weeks on end. But he need not complain perpetually.

The value of training in administration can be seen in the

matter of use of time. Some of the time consumed in the work of the pastor is due to inefficient administration. Time can be saved by efficient administration of a program and a part of that time belongs legitimately to the man who saved it. It belongs to the minister and his family. The ability to decide quickly between that which is important and that which is essential and then to be content with leaving some things neglected is a skill that a minister needs to develop.

There are men in the ministry who are very insecure. Sometimes these are men who went through college, through seminary, and into the ordained ministry with no stop off in "business" or in the armed services. These are sometimes the ones who suffer from anxiety because there is no back door out of their vocational choice. There is no other field of labor for which they are equipped, and they are afraid within their chosen field. There is talk in some circles about the necessity of helping some of these who are most anxious to "retool." This would make it possible for them to go into some other field of labor.

A part of this problem is caused by a lack of attention to the training of men in administration. There is a refusal to admit the secular nature of the church. Classical studies still hold the center of the stage in seminary training. When a man gets out, he may flounder in despair for years. Then he needs to be retooled in order to escape. For a man to be trained in administration is not necessarily going to spoil him for the ministry. It may simply free him for the ministry. The continuing complaint that a man has not time enough to study should be attacked in the real church. To set aside arbitrarily a time that is sacred for study is not sufficient. The administrative task of the minister is a fact of life. The only way in which he can solve it in the real world is to attack it with vigor and efficiency. After that task has been dispatched he can then turn to study or recreation or to what he considers to be the useful tasks of counseling and teaching.

If a man were trained in the facts of secular life and admin-

istration, even if he did leave the ministry, he might not need
"retooling." He could, perhaps, be more content and secure
in his vocation as a pastor and, if he had to escape, he would
be able to move into another secular vocation outside the
church because he was already equipped for it.

The work of administration is associated with the role of
the minister. He should be thankful for this association. If
he will do his task with as much skill and care and efficiency
as he can muster, he will have some basis for identification
with the members of his parish who also work in the secular
world.

A Ministry of Social Concern

"If the young minister looks for the most difficult and most
dangerous post for the proclaiming of a gospel that grapples
with the real issues besetting mankind today, he will volun-
teer for suburban service. The difficulty is the baffling intran-
sigence of the people. The danger is that such a minister will
either be corrupted by the lush climate in which he operates
or be fired before he can become effective. The young minister who believes that the gospel has to do with rescuing
men from war, racism, drug addiction, filthy slums, poverty,
unemployment — with the whole gamut of human misery and
degradation — will discover that the inner city parish is a
picnic compared with the suburban church. Relevant? No
ministry is more relevant than one challenging those men and
women who consciously or unconsciously champion the con-
ditions producing human misery and degradation far from
their own homes and churches. Effective? Well, that is
another matter; but the young minister can at least have a
try at it. The rescue operation demanded of the church in
the inner city will never end unless someone attempts a preventive operation in the suburbs. In the safe, comfortable,
affluent suburb the young minister who takes Christ's mission

to the whole world seriously risks his soul or his job —
sometimes both. But that kind of ministry isn't dull, or irrelevant, or wholly effective." [7]

These pages are addressed primarily to the parish minister.
The man in a paraparochial situation has a different set of
problems and must take a completely different approach to
the matter of interpreting his role and image. His task is complicated. We are concerned here with the man who lives
within the vulnerable fishbowl of the parish.

My contention is that the parish minister is in a position
to be far more creative in the expression of social concern
than any other professonal. By witness to social concern, I
mean not only preaching but real participation in politics,
marching, or civil rights demonstrations. Part of the weight
of his witness is due to his vulnerable position. He can be
shot down by any number of sections of the gallery. This
does not mean that he is to run headlong into martyrdom. Few
are really marked for that special crown. Martyrdom is not
achieved without a lifetime of intense and calculated living
witness. The young minister who blasts off on some social issue
in his first parish bears no martyr's crown. He has simply
wasted his opportunity.

No witness on a vital social issue on the part of a local pastor will have creative effect until that man has earned the
respect of the core of his congregation. If his witness is pre-
mature, that is, if it is brought to the level of burning issue
before he has earned the respect of his congregation, he may
be shot down in a blaze of misunderstanding. If the congregation does not grasp what he is saying or doing in his witness,
then he has failed to influence the very persons for whom he has
accepted responsibility. It takes time to make yourself clear to
all of the group. If a man fails to wait until a significant proportion of the people understand him, he will simply be inef-
fective. If a minister is "loved" too sentimentally by his
people, they will tolerate him as a sentimental dreamer. They

will not take him seriously. If he is not loved at all, he will be rejected out of hand and his total impact as a witness will be negated.

It is sometimes professional irresponsibility for a minister to run so counter to the image and expectations of his congregation that he is removed from his pastorate. This can happen in churches of congregational polity and sometimes does. Ministers in denominations with a polity that offers a more protected status to the minister are sometimes more free to give witness to social concerns. Their office as pastor is not quite as vulnerable as in the congregational polity. The ineffectiveness of these ministers may stem from the fact that they are not understood, are sentimentally tolerated, or have not earned the respect of their people.

It is the professional responsibility of a pastor to judge the distance between himself and the people he leads. If he gets too far ahead, he may lose contact. He must learn to speak clearly and specifically as well. A witness to some social concern that is couched in theological language or in generalities is both safe and irrelevant. If he is willing to be specific, the minister will be forced to make peace with a position that is only partly right.

There is a pointed illustration of the opaque generalized social witness in a powerful section of Albert Camus' final volume, *Resistance, Rebellion, and Death.* Camus, an avowed atheist, is addressing the sisters of a Roman Catholic convent at the close of World War II. He had spent the years of the war risking his life in the resistance movement of France. " For a long time during those frightful years I waited for a great voice to speak up in Rome. I, an unbeliever? Precisely. For I knew that the spirit would be lost if it did not utter a cry of condemnation when faced with force. It seems that that voice did speak up. But I assure you that millions of men like me did not hear it and that at that time believers and unbelievers alike shared a solitude that continued to spread as the days went by and the executioners multiplied.

It has been explained to me since that the condemnation was indeed voiced. But that it was in the style of the encyclicals, which is not at all clear." [8] The pastor should speak as specifically as possible.

The professional responsibility of the pastor is to hold the congregation together long enough to gain a real hearing. This may make it necessary for him to conform to some of the false images of the members of his congregation. It may be necessary to perform tasks that seem irrelevant and useless to him. But he has accepted a professional responsibility to that congregation and if he is going to be heard, he must maintain the contact long enough to gain the needed respect or his witness will be useless to those who are his special responsibility.

He is to avoid arrogance. He should have some sense of history. The issue that was clear twenty years ago is now qualified by history. If a man is 51 percent right in his witness to social concern, he is on the side of the angels. Each decision or stand must be examined on its own merit. In a contextual situation there is no black or white. It is the responsibility of the professional to be on the side which is least gray. But this fact cannot paralyze a man. He must be willing to be wrong. If he is not willing to be wrong, he cannot relate his theology to real decisions. His belief must remain a glorious but meaningless generality. Clearly, however, no arrogance is justified. A humble firmness is appropriate.

The ministry is the last vocation in which a man has enough freedom to tear a week out of his datebook and go to Selma. The image which he carries along with him into that situation is still capable of calling up real reaction. To wear a clerical collar in some parts of the nation in 1967 is dangerous. No vocation can be irrelevant if it can elicit the response of hatred simply by being. Other professions participate in such movements, but the minister is the one who is spat upon.

It is professional responsibility to know the issue, to keep contact with the people and earn their respect, to be specific and risk being wrong, to avoid arrogance and to risk one's person in meaningful witness to social concern.

A Ministry to the Future

The future is upon us. We can respond to it on two levels. First, as an earth-shaking or a theology-shaking set of new categories. This seems to be rather naïve because speed of change hardly has theological meaning. What is changed? The prestige of empirical science is increased but its stock has already been high for a long time. Secondly, we can respond by recognition that the ministry of the pastor is going to be much more complicated in the next ten years than it has been in the past. This is the more significant fact of life.

We ought to be impressed by the achievements of science and technology. The escalation of speed, population, and knowledge should put us as churchmen in a stance of expectancy, and we should meet the challenge of the future in the most vigorous way. But the whole idea of transcendence that is under fire in the sixties has been questioned with passion since the latter part of the eleventh century. Empirical science has been challenging the church with vigor for generations.

The fact of life is that we still live in a world where love and joy and pain and birth and death are real. Persons put on these facts of life daily, and we are called to minister to persons through our own humanity — through our own love and joy and pain and death.

The future is upon us, and we are faced with the facts which that future brings to life. As a matter of fact, the future is passing us by.

Fifteen years ago, a fact of the future impinged itself upon the ministry of a man. A family of the congregation discovered that their little baby was a seriously impaired spastic. In a year of prayer and counsel, the pastor discovered that the child had been born as a result of artificial insemination by a donor. The anxiety and guilt that were carried by husband and wife both were a vastly complicating factor in the whole family dynamic. To have a child who has a birth defect is complex enough, but under the impact of the supposed contribution of modern medicine, it is far more so. This is not to say that artificial insemination was the source of the defect. Probably it had nothing to do with the spastic condition of the child. The complicating fact was that the human decision of this family had injected a new factor into the cycle of love and joy and birth and death. Our ministry in the future is going to be far more complicated than before by these injections of the future.

The situation described took place fifteen years ago. In the year 1961 the conservative estimate of children born through artificial insemination was 100,000. The pace has escalated rapidly.

The General Assembly of the United Presbyterian Church has met every year and made pronouncements on social and moral issues but the subject of artificial insemination has yet to be touched. Artificial insemination hasn't been future for twenty years: it has been present.

There is no question but that the social revolution holds center stage at the moment. It belongs there. The escalation of our world into future will have an effect upon that social revolution. We really do not have enough wisdom to assess whether the effect will be predominantly positive or negative. We can only say that technology will make the ghetto a different place. But we do not know if it will be better or worse due to technology.

The transplanting of kidneys and the artificial regulation of hearts will mean complicated decisions for physicians and all persons. If we have wisdom, we are bound to contribute as we can. The reality is that even with an artificially regulated heartbeat a person will still function within the cycle of love and joy and pain and birth and death. We will still live in a world where resurrection takes place, where Jesus was raised and we are candidates for resurrection. Either this, or we will live in a world where there is no resurrection.

The decisions that are bound to be forced upon us by the advances of technology are minor compared with the social revolution that is taking place at the present time. The whole structure of society is being reshaped. The mores that have been the keel of the generations past are being reexamined as never before. The population explosion has implications that no one has yet assessed. Theology is in ferment. The information explosion will change the whole picture of education within the next ten years. Vocations are no longer thought of as lifetime callings. We are being told that men in technical work will be required to retool for another whole vocation every ten years in the coming generation.

Add to all of this the threat of atomic warfare and the racial tension that seems to be on the rise all over the world, and the fact becomes plain that the future is really here.

This book is not a self-help book designed to help pastors "find their true selfhood." Rather, it is addressed to a present problem: the fact that the pastor carries an image of authority and elicits certain expectations from those whom he contacts. Personally, I would hope that the whole subject will become quickly obsolete and irrelevant because the image has either faded or become meaningful. But meanwhile it is critical for the pastor to use his image properly or he can be assured that others will use it for their own purposes.

The pastor is called to be a mature and competent experimenter. It is a part of his professional responsibility to lead the church into the future. He must be willing to risk his own status and in some cases his comfort in searching out relevance for the church.

Here is an illustration of one of the ways a church tries to meet one of the problems mentioned above, that of mobility. As the church has moved into the sixties, there is less and less enthusiasm among laymen and pastors for keeping the parish machinery going. It just does not seem all that important to keep the groups and committees and classes and clubs functioning. People come into the church seeking meaning and relevance and ministry and they frequently end with leadership responsibility in jobs that are pleasant, social, and " religious " but seem to have no real purpose. We are conscious of an urgency in our generation. Lots of people are just plain scared. Others are deeply concerned about the real world of poverty and pain and feel a reluctance to waste time in meaningless wheel-oiling and church-centered busywork.

Besides all of this, there are an increasing number of churches that are utterly frantic from the fact of continual population turnover. No sooner is a teacher or an elder trained than he is transferred or moves. It is not in the least unusual in some parts of the United States for a congregation to turn over completely in a space of five years. As a matter of fact, this is the national average. Actually, the turnover is much faster and a church often has contact with a person for six months to two years, with few staying for more than a year.

There is a positive reaction to this problem and it has direct relation to the stance of the pastor. His attitude to this fact of fluidity can be creative or destructive, and it will be reflected in the morale of the parish.

In a small West Coast church which is faced with this fluidity, a creative step is taken. The people who go out of the individual parish always go somewhere, and it is appropriate that, as they leave a church family, they be commissioned. We should say good-by properly.

In the course of two years in this particular parish, it said a formal farewell to four elders. One went on a tour of duty as an officer in Vietnam, one went to another city to begin a new business venture, one went to Chile to work as an engineer on a road survey, and one went to Venezuela as a State Department consultant in municipal government. In addition to this, there were others who left. One went to Washington,

D.C., as an attorney for AID; another, a young architect, sold everything he had and went to Europe with his wife and baby to travel until his money ran out.

The formal farewell was a part of morning worship on the last Sunday the family could be present. They were called forward in the service, a word was said about their "new ministry" or the meaning of their new responsibility, and they were commissioned to their new task in the world. The expectation is that they will be active churchmen where they go. They are not missionaries or satellites of one congregation.

In this particular church, each family was given a used hymnal out of the pew rack. New hymnals are purchased to make up for the drain on the old ones. The book means more if it shows the marks of the hands of friends. Sometimes a reception was held after the service. One of the elders mentioned above was city manager, and the city council, the mayor, and other leaders of the community were invited to a reception following morning worship.

In itself, this public recognition of the movement within a church is a simple device. But it offers the pastor a chance to communicate important concepts by his stance. He affirms the validity of each man's vocation as a Christian vocation in this way. He is able to speak the affection of the congregation and to remind everyone present of our relationship to all Christians. Within a few years, a network of significant ties with persons around the world can be built even for a small congregation.

A key to all this is the stance and attitude of the minister. If he spends his life grousing about the flow or complaining about training elders for other churches, he will never participate creatively in this fact of the future. If he is positive and creative about the meaning of this often frustrating mobility of the parish, he can lead the whole congregation to a similar attitude. It can become a window into the world.

The call to think new thoughts and experiment with new ministries is not an option. Those in the profession of the ministry have no alternative but to seek new ways to speak to this generation. Responsible experimentation is the only way in which the church will achieve any relevance.

The Minister as Educator

One of the more frustrating areas of the professional life of the minister is his role as educator. His training is essentially that of a teacher. Yet this is one of the functions which he frequently finds must be set aside because of the other demands made upon his time. His work with the church school is frequently a job of recruitment and administration. If he is fortunate enough to have members of the congregation who do this work efficiently, he may be removed to the category of consultant to a committee on Christian education. This is useful but it is not always teaching. The teaching function of a consultant is limited.

Wesner Fallaw, of Andover Newton Theological Seminary, has come forth with a thesis that ought not to be revolutionary but seems to be so. He suggests that since the minister is the trained person in the congregation, he should be the teacher. This idea, which is at least as old as the designation " rabbi " in the Judeo-Christian world, may take hold in the church again.

In the last few years more pastors have been getting into direct contact with the people on a teaching base. There has been an increased use of a " talk back " session following morning worship. At times, these sessions become " dialogue " within the worship service itself. The " talk back " can involve someone other than the minister as leader. It may be a freer discussion if he is not present. But if the dialogue is to be a mutual learning experience for the minister and the congregation, it is important that he be involved in the actual conversation. The " talk back" is an efficient method of discovering what people hear in a sermon, but it can be discouraging. It can also be very useful in pointing out the areas where communication really takes place.

Dialogue is often threatening to the minister. If he is not able to grant beforehand that the ideas he presents may not seem important or relevant to the congregation, he is threatened. He may discover that the people heard something entirely different from what he intended. Or he may discover that they have missed his point.

It is probably useless to repreach the sermon. It is not the sermon that really matters. The minister may feel better if he is assured that he has been understood. But his own feelings are not the important matter. The issue at hand is the need of the listener. It is questionable whether the understanding of the sermon is going to be a means of grace. Preaching is grasped by the hearer by handles that are almost completely subjective. There is a tendency to hear what is being listened for. The minister who has not been in dialogue may forget this fact.

Another advantage to such dialogue is that sometimes the basic ideas of the minister come under attack. He can have a defensive attitude or an open appreciation of this challenge. It is possible for him to admit that he does not have answers to all the questions brought forward by the congregation. He can turn to others in the congregation and ask for their views on the problem. When he does this, he is admitting his fallibility and is liable to discover a new attitude in his congregation. He may have the threatening prospect of being openly questioned in other areas of the church's life. (The questioning has always been there, covertly, anyway, but it may now come into the open.) At the same time, he may become a more useful pastor because he is regarded as a more " human figure." If he does not know all the answers, he is certainly human. This new attitude may serve to make others more free to converse usefully with the minister.

Here again he should have a grasp of the relation between faith and life. If he does not see a particular relation clearly, he had best admit this failing. For example, he may have no ready answer to a real moral question that is raised in the dialogue. It may be impossible to cite chapter and verse to establish a moral position even if the pastor is a legalist. If he opens the discussion by referring to the situational ethic as basic, he can establish a rationale for a whole series of potentially harmful decisions. If he is rigid, he may only establish a point against which revolt can take place.

It is possible to involve others in the conversation and to seek guidelines within the group. It is possible to reveal a somewhat rigid moral response and acknowledge its limitations with candor. Ultimately, if the issue is real, the person asking the question will make up his own mind. It is neither safe nor kind to be so oblique in reply that a clever rationalizer gets support for some act he will later regret having taken.

There are times when the candid admission of humanity by the minister is threatening to the congregation. They would prefer to bask under the illusion that the minister is wise. An admission of fallibility can become the beginning of growth for all parties concerned. The mutual growth in understanding of role can begin then on a more meaningful base.

There is another sign of hope in this connection. Currently there is a revived interest in a weekday church school. One of the happy things about this revival is the increasing role of the minister as teacher. It seems highly appropriate for the pastor to be a teacher of children as well as of adults. In the past three years, the church that I have served has turned to a weekday church school. Such a school has many advantages. It is held on a weekday after school. It follows the academic year of the public schools and therefore presents to children the image of a real educational enterprise. The recruitment of teachers is easier for this hour of the week because adults are more available. In addition, it has a blessed tendency to alleviate the Sunday morning rush for many families.

Attendance percentages in the weekday church school tend to be much higher than Sunday morning school because the weekday does not interfere with family plans. This is likely to be a more significant factor as the amount of available leisure time increases. The family in which the father works four days each week, instead of five or five and a half days, will increase during the coming decade. Recreation will increase and many more families will be taken out of the community for the weekend. Family recreation can be of great value in terms of its positive effect on family unity. It would be a sad thing for the church to try to hold back in order to keep the children in Sunday church school. A weekday church school can be as useful as one held on Sunday. Actually, it can be more useful.

More time can be allowed for teaching on a weekday. If pupils will come to the church at the end of their day at public school, they can arrive by three or three-thirty in the afternoon. If they are given a cookie and a little punch, they can survive until five. A touch of sugar is very important and ought not to be neglected. If they can have cookies and a brief period of corporate worship before four o'clock, there remains a full hour for teaching. Teacher-pupil ratio can be reduced so that there is more real contact between teacher and pupil.

The minister can be fully involved as a teacher and leader of worship in the school. He then is able to be closer to the children and to be available to them. A secondary gain is in his own attitude and learning. Children can utterly disarm any of us. They are capable, simply by their presence, of reducing questions to reality. There is opportunity to be intellectually seduced by adults. Adult questions that are complex and interesting can be wonderful hiding places from reality. Frequently, these are the kinds of questions adults will ask. But children ask simple questions and thus make the task of answering far more demanding. They are far more difficult to answer than adults.

When children see the minister as a leader in worship and a teacher, they will respond to him in a particular way. If he carries himself with openness and humility, he may avoid the awe-inspiring image that he can so easily assume in the eyes of children. Even if he does inspire their awe, or assume a deeper authority than he would like to carry, this does not mean that his usefulness to the children is destroyed. It only means that he must be more careful because he has more authority. Lots of people report their earliest experience with a minister in somewhat awesome terms. He is pictured as an unbending, white-haired saint, aloof and humorless. This is not what the average minister wants as an image. But even this rigid saint may have had positive influence in the life of the person who reports the experience. At least, he has established a point of reference. Perhaps it was a reference point for revolt. But it was stable, predictable, and took human shape. Children see adults from a perspective that makes the grown-up loom large. The added strangeness that attaches to the minister can make a child see a very large body indeed.

The possibility of transmitting real humanity is increased with increased contact. "A child or adolescent no less than an adult deserves to have direct and very personal contact with his minister. Children are eager for recognition and support by the pastor, not superficially but at a genuine pastoral level. They stand ready to respond to him, if he proves that he has an affinity for them, for as we have already noted they want a significant person — to use the current phrase — to relate to, to admire, to look up to. More often than adults perhaps, they are quick to identify themselves with a person of recognized merit. For those in middle childhood and adolescence, a man of God is needed; and for many younger children, a woman of God." [9]

The young clergyman or seminary student frequently feels a horror of looming large in the eyes of children and young people. He does not want to be threatening or authoritative. Working with young people of junior high and high school age is the cause of much anxiety on the part of ministers. They often feel incapable of working with them adequately and try to avoid contact. Many younger men will find they are "successful" in relating to youth if they reject the image of the minister completely and simply step back into the role of youth. They may arrive at the seminary as experienced youth workers or as leaders in this generation's particular revolt of youth. By the time they enter a parish, they are tired of "youth work." This sometimes means that they want to be with adults and to teach adults. The habit of relating to youth as semiadolescents has become very tiresome for them and they look forward to the adult world. If they can achieve a church with a multiple staff they are likely to turn youth work over to their youngest assistant.

It is not right for the minister to desert the young people simply because he feels unable to identify with them. The pastor of the church belongs with the children and the young people. It is not really important for him to be well liked. It may be helpful but it is not essential. It *is* important for him to be consistent, predictable, and clear. He should give genuine indication that he is interested in young people. It is not necessary for a minister to act like a teen-ager in order to give the impression of interest. Actually, adolescent behavior on his part is an effective way to eliminate his potential leadership. Relating to children and youth requires particular care in the positive use of professional identity.

The whole problem of a relationship to children is complicated. It is particularly confusing when the adult carries a role with a connotation of authority. Willard Waller makes the observation that this relationship requires a sort of alternation of attitudes. Waller is speaking of teachers in particular, but the same observations have validity for the minister who acts as a teacher with children. "Thus one says, 'I am your teacher' in a certain unemotional tone of the voice. This begets discipline, perhaps some sullenness, certainly emotional and personal frustration on the part of both student and teacher. Before this reaction has been carried through to completion, one says, 'But I am a human being and I try to be a good fellow. And you are all fine people and we have some good times together, don't we?' This is role number two, and if taken at its face value, it begets a desirable cheerfulness and a dangerous friendliness. If he carries too long upon this grace note, the teacher loses his authority by becoming a member of the group. He must revert to role number one, and say, with just a hint of warning and implication of adult dignity in his voice, 'But I am the teacher.' All this occurs a hundred times a day in every school room and it marks the rhythm of the teacher's movements of advancement and retreat with reference to his students, the alternate expansion and contraction of his personality. It does not occur, of course, in so obvious a form as this; it is perhaps only the very unskillful teacher who needs to put such things into words." [10]

One of the principal characteristics of those who find their way into the ministry is that they want to be loved by all. It is not nearly so necessary to be loved as it is to be useful. It is the professional responsibility of the minister to be useful to young people, to children, and to adults.

The local minister has another role as educator. He has opportunity to be a real influence in the public schools of the community. One of the experiences I have had in the smaller communities where I have served is being taken seriously by educators. The minister is generally thought of as a man of culture and education. He is often called upon by local school boards to assist in the study of goals or as a special consultant. When he is invited to take part in this sort of work by the school officials, he may be surprised at the amount of weight he carries as a community figure. Even in the West, where the clergyman is tolerated with various degrees of enthusiasm, he will find that when he speaks on an educational issue people tend to listen.

The pastor of the local church should be very close to the public schools. He should take advantage of this "educator image" and do what he can as a creative influence in the school system.

The Matter of Compensation (Salary)

If we take seriously what has been said about the secular nature of the church and the professional nature of the ministry, there are some important implications in the area of salaries for ministers. But it is dangerous to say much about the matter of salary for ministers without making some qualifying comments at the beginning.

The concept of service as an aspect of the profession of ministry is critically important. Unless a man has a motivation to serve others, he is out of place in any of the helping professions. This is particularly true of the ministry. It is possible to analyze a great deal of the motivation of the average minister and discover that he has desires which imply a doubt about his altruism. Many a minister has gone through this painful experience. He may discover that he has a need to be needed by others. He may feel that his greatest good is to be heard or martyred for his faith or for some social stance. Or he may have a passion to "serve God" which is called paranoid by others. He may even conclude in some black mood that his motives are so colored by other factors that there is no altruism or real love left in his person.

Yet all of this analysis can fail to account for his real drive toward a useful role in the church, the community, and in the lives of other people. If he is concerned about persons enough to enter the ministry in the first place, he can act upon the faith that real love does exist within him. It may require a continuing act of faith for him to accept this. Perhaps it can be used by God simply because it is an act of faith. A sense of concern is essential and, in the overwhelming majority of cases, the minister is genuinely motivated by this concern. How does this concern for others, coupled with the secular nature of his profession, influence the minister's attitude toward his salary?

The whole issue hinges on the base that the minister uses for making significant choices. Every professional makes a deliberate choice and at times he pays for this choice in substance. A medical doctor who chooses to do research or to teach in the medical school has made a choice that may mean that his income will be less than it could be in private practice. If he chooses to work in a large medical group, he has also made a choice that may limit his income. It may be that he will be spared some of the headaches of private practice. He has no problem of arriving at fees and making billings, and he may be able to practice what he considers to be better medicine. Nevertheless, he has made a choice. He has chosen one type of practice instead of another. He has made that choice partly on the basis of his professional responsibility and his interest, and partly on the basis of his potential income.

In the same way, a minister will make choices. If he decides upon a special ministry in which he relates to a denominational board instead of a congregation, he may have avoided some aspects of congregational life. He may also have limited his variety of contacts and probably his salary. He may be faced with monthly reports to a board in New York City, and he may be faced with conservative board members or a demanding supervisor. He has made a choice.

A minister may have opportunity to move to a larger and better paying position in another congregation. If the work in the particular congregation he serves is at a critical point, he must question his right to move. Even though his income is an important factor in his family life, he must make his choice on the basis of both his professional responsibility and his pocketbook. If he is a responsible professional, then the good of the congregation takes an important position alongside the necessity for an increase in income. It is also possible that a man may frankly desire to stay with a smaller congregation rather than move to a larger church. In this case, again, he makes a deliberate choice.

These comments apply most directly to those members of denominations in which a man moves freely upon invitation. If he has chosen a denomination in which he works under a bishop or a district superintendent, this means that he has made his choice at this initial point in his career.

There comes a time in the life of most ministers when the demands of family responsibilities necessitate a serious concern about an increase in income. There is no reason why he should make his family suffer. If he serves in a church that is secular and if his profession is secular, it is appropriate to serve as other professionals do. His choices should be based to some degree on his professional responsibility and on the basis of interest. Yet he can and should regard his family responsibilities. He ought also to consider his skills as a salable commodity. There is no reason why he cannot look upon his ability as a fund raiser, or administrator, or counselor, as a usefulness which he has for sale. It is proper that he work to improve these salable skills with the objective of increasing his usefulness *and* his income as well. It is proper for a minister to study administration, or fund-raising, or counseling with the deliberate purpose of increasing both his skills and his income.

If a man goes to a position at a salary he considers to be too small, he may feel put upon from the very beginning. This will not produce a healthful attitude toward his work. In the printed call which is used by some denominations, it is stated that the compensation is given in order to make it possible for the pastor to be " free from all worldly cares and avocations." This has been inferred to mean that the responsibility of the congregation is to keep the minister and his family from worldly cares. This is not necessarily the way it works out. There are times when a man may have the attitude that the church is some sort of mother who is committed to care for her children. This attitude will seldom get a raise in salary.

The laborer is worthy of his hire. It is dignified for a man to look upon his professional capacities as worth enough for him to live in comfort and to send his children through college. It is honest for a man to look for the maximum salary he can command. This expectation must be tempered by a real sense of professional responsibility. The deliberate choices that a minister makes must be based upon where he should serve for the best interests of the visible church. When he has needs that cannot be met in a particular parish, he has the option of looking for a more adequate parish. But he is never free from his professional responsibility for the visible church in which he serves. If he assesses the situation and concludes that he is free to move, then it is proper to consider his skills as being worthy of compensation.

He is always subject to rationalization. There may be a gross exaggeration of his worth to the visible body in which he works. He may make a miscalculation as to the extent to which he has "finished the job." It is possible that he may have overestimated the opposition to the program he feels is important in the parish he serves at present. These rationalizations can cloud the issue and the only hope for objectivity is proper professional appraisal of all aspects of a man's work and his skills.

This sounds rather cold-blooded, yet it need not be so. With a proper perspective on professional responsibility, family responsibility, and a man's own tolerance for tension, a minister can achieve some objectivity. Excessive ambition or greed may complicate a man's decision-making process. But assuming that greedy and ambitious men will find more lucrative vocations, and emphasizing the need for a spirit of service, it is proper to say that a minister should not work without satisfactory compensation.

A Ministry to Fellow Ministers

There is a longing on the part of most ministers for candidness and openness with other ministers. The Wednesday luncheon group of clergymen is not at all unusual. Most ministers are thrown together in the conference, or the diocese, or the presbytery with men of their own denomination and they do have a chance to visit. Frequently, they will seek out interdenominational relationships as well. At times, close and deep friendships which were begun in seminary days can continue through the years.

These contacts are at various levels of intensity. Sometimes close friendships develop. Other times there are too many barriers to relationship, and the contact is doomed to superficiality. It may be that a man has taken refuge too deeply inside the protective cover of his professional identity. It may be that the inner politics of the denomination structure to which the various ministers belong inhibits the relationship. There may be jealousy among the ministers or envy of one another. Differences in salaries, differences in socioeconomic levels of parishes, geographic location, or various degrees of achievement can all be the seedbed for envy. This is not to say that associations between ministers are not good or healthy but it should be recognized that they are seldom pure " koinonia." As a result, they suffer the limitation that comes from recognizing one another as failing human beings.

Usually this same set of limitations will extend to the minister's family. They may have friends on a far deeper level than other people have friendships. Nevertheless they are not living as Christian friends in a state of perpetual " agape." As a result, ministers and their families are in need of adequate professional care.

There are times of crisis and loss in the lives of ministers and their families. They are no different in this respect from any other group. But in time of loss, or hospitalization, or pain, it is rare for a minister or his family to receive professional care from another minister. They may get friendly calls in the hospital, but it is rare for the minister or his wife, or his child, to get a *pastoral* call. I would plead for this type of ministry.

A professional hospital call is one in which the patient is approached with a recognition of the fact of the validity of the church's ministry to him. Many years ago I was laid up with a severe infection and spent a lot of time in pain in the hospital. Work was neglected, worries about money impinged, worries about long-range health and other things were much on my mind. People called, they sent flowers, they brought food. But the most impressive thing that happened was the visit of a neighboring pastor who came, visited seriously, read a psalm, and said a prayer. He was a close friend and one with whom I had much in common. We had joked together, camped together, and eaten in each other's homes. But for a few moments he set aside the face of friendship and became a professional. This was much appreciated at the time and has influenced my attitude toward this opportunity for ministry ever since.

This type of ministry has to be handled with great care. It can be deliberately stated to the individual that the visit is professional. Even though he may be a fellow minister or the wife of a fellow pastor, it is perfectly appropriate to indicate that you are there in a professional capacity. There is not any reason why an old friendship cannot be the base for a helpful conversation. There is also no reason why a minister's family should be denied the potential help of an adequate ministry.

Being professional does not mean that the minister puts on his piety and goes through a routine. It means that he sets aside his role as friend for a bit and becomes a minister to this minister. He has the same listening attitude as he would have in calling on a parishioner. He follows the lead of the patient but he represents the church and the gospel of resurrection.

This may seem to be a potentially embarrassing assignment. It may be. But it is useful to individuals. It is useful to persons who are often denied some things simply because they are professionals or families related to professionals.

Chapter 5

The Uses of Authority in the Role

He that negotiates between God and man,
As God's ambassador, the grand concerns
Of judgment and of mercy, should beware
Of lightness in his speech.
— William Cowper, *The Task,*
Book II, line 463.

The nature of the authority that is associated with the role of the minister varies with the age of the image holder. It varies according to the part of the country from which that person originates, the amount of education, and, of course, the denominational background. There are so many variables that it seems impossible to make any general statement about the nature of the minister's authority.

Each minister carries a varying authority into every relationship. This is affected by his own carriage of his person, his education, and the background against which he projects himself. With some, it is a mystical authority. With some, the authority will be limited to esoteric knowledge. With others, the authority of personhood will count for the most. In any case, the minister will always carry with him certain authority. The question is how to use it creatively.

There are dangers attached to the exercise of this psychic weight. Something that has been accepted on another person's authority and then disproved will have the effect of destroying the original relationship along with the old opinion. Therefore, if an inquiring person can be encouraged to think through the matter for himself, everyone is better off. The minister who carries too much weight is also going to carry the burden of violent rejection at times.

The authority of the pastor can and is used by other persons to justify their own behavior. Suppose a person is in doubt about whether he is doing the proper thing in a given situation. He is having an affair. He has rationalized the business but still has doubts. He may seek out the pastor, seeking reinforcement of his rationalization process. Some who come with this motive can be quite blunt about their need. " I am doing something which society considers to be bad. As I look at it, and under such and such circumstances, it does not seem to be evil. What do you think, pastor? Don't you feel that I am justified? "

A wife may come to complain about her husband's behavior. " He is unreasonable. Last week he stayed out until two A.M. Don't you feel that this is wrong? " The pastor is faced with this sort of question and has only a Rogerian technique to fall back upon. If he does insist on the individual's dealing with his or her own problem, the minister will arouse anxiety and he will frequently arouse anger. But if he agrees or disagrees with the value judgment that has been expressed, he may lose his usefulness altogether.

In the area of value judgment, many people will try to use the authority attached to the office of the minister. They will try to use it to justify themselves or to condemn others. The minister should learn to use that authority himself instead of allowing it to be used by others. This was not so difficult when the moral code was more rigid, specific, and accepted. The minister then could express a basic agreement with certain moral standards and be free from manipulation. However, if ethics is considered to be a dynamic decision-making process within the context of life rather than a rigid code, the problem is much more difficult. The minister can refer the person back to the context and insist that he make up his own mind in the light of the situation and the demands of love. In doing this, he is allowing himself to be drawn into a deeper consideration of the problem. It is easier for the minister to be a representative of a theoretical moral position. At times it may also be more useful to the person involved for the minister to maintain this sort of position.

If making a moral decision is really the essence of a struggling man's problem, he will have to make the decision for himself. He may be helped by having a rigid standard to which he can relate. He may end by dismissing or rejecting that standard. But it may be helpful to have a theoretical reference point. In many cases where people struggle with decisions, the moral issue is not the essence. The calls of expedience and profit are strong. The search may really be for a way of rationalizing the matter so that the decider can live with his decision.

If, under these circumstances, the minister uses his authority to lead this seeker into an examination of the problem from the point of view of situation ethics, he may multiply the possibilities for rationalization. He may make the solution that was originally desired easier to arrive at. This does not mean that the decider is free of feelings of guilt. He may still have the residue of guilt which results from what may be his own inner standards. When a minister uses his authority to guide someone into a more dynamic and sophisticated area of situation ethics, he may have accomplished nothing but additional frustration.

The image of the minister as moral authority is not necessarily always negative. When the clergyman decides to step beyond a code and to try to lead his counselee to a more creative and dynamic ethic, he should make some judgment as to what his counselee is seeking. If that counselee is looking for rationale for doing what is expedient, then the minister may conclude that he should remain a moral authority. If he is faced with a person who is really seeking to do the right thing, then the minister may decide to help to teach a more dynamic ethical process.

The task of the pastor is to use the authority image that he carries as a professional and to use it properly. If he does not use it properly, it will be used by others who may be no wiser than he and possibly less so. It is his by virtue of his profession, and he is therefore responsible for its use.

The uses made of other aspects of the authority image are complex. If the minister comes to a hospital room where he is expected to pray, it is appropriate that he do so. His theology of prayer may be highly refined. He may abhor the idea that his own prayer could carry more weight than another person's prayer. This may be true in God's eyes and in truth. But this still does not mean that the minister is bound to demur — to give over the time of prayer to teaching. There will possibly be a time when he can teach this expectant person something more about the true nature of prayer. When that person lies on a hospital bed in pain, it is not the appropriate time for this sort of lesson. The pastor should do what is expected of him and look for a chance to teach another day.

One of the traps into which a minister can be snared is being called upon to settle an argument or a dispute. He is called in to be an authority. Disputes of this kind can range from quarrels about " What does the Bible say? " to deeply personal quarrels. The minister must first estimate the depth of the dispute and then decide whether it is appropriate to enter as authority. If it is a simple matter of whether a verse appears in the Bible or where it appears, he may take advantage of this little boost to his ego with good conscience. This is one of the few rewards he may ever get for studying Hebrew and Greek.

But if it is a deeper personal quarrel, he may take a tip from Solomon and force those persons back on themselves. He may stand at the side to help bring about a reconciliation, but to step into the situation and become involved as a judge is probably fruitless. In the use of the authority image, the minister is called to be as calculating and careful as possible. This is the way in which he can be most loving and useful. The dangers in the authority role are obvious and uncomfortable. Using the positive values of that authority requires a great deal of imagination.

The Necessity for Self-examination

In all of this there is a profound necessity for continuing self-examination. A man must do this for himself. He cannot rely on others for the evaluation of his ministry. Appreciative little old ladies will always be available to butter his ego. The denomination tends to honor and uphold the "successful" pastor. The problem is that he may be successful precisely because he is cautious, clever, manipulative, and "professional" in the pejorative sense.

The man who takes risks with his image may do so because he is hounded by self-destructive neuroses. He may, on the other hand, take those risks because of concern for people and faith in the resurrection. He may believe that God is able to raise the church from the dead if it takes risks in its own life. He may believe that if he takes his own professional risks seriously and for the right reasons, he is a candidate for resurrection. The appropriate stance for a man who believes in the resurrection is the stance of a risking person. He should ask himself frequently, "Am I risking anything?"

The counsel contained in these pages sets forth a dangerous doctrine. It is suggested that the minister be deliberate and calculating in the use of the burden he carries.

Two dangers emerge: one, that the minister will take this advice to heart and become hardened to the hope that he needs to keep alive. It is possible to slip from a useful, professional stance into a comfortable and cynical attitude toward everything. In a sense, he sets his goal much lower when he looks to the church as a secular institution and regards his own work as professional rather than a holy vocation. This, in a time when goals everywhere seem dangerously low already, represents a danger. The real danger is the paralyzing cynicism that can overtake a man who regards his work as a thorough professional. Somehow a healthy tension between *what is* and *what might be* must be kept alive. No secular community is beyond improvement. The church has potential growth in its usefulness as a tool for mission. There must be faith on the part of the minister that the church can be used. This is his guard against cynicism.

The second danger is manifold. This is the danger that he might so miscalculate his role in the eyes of others that he hinders their growth instead of stimulating that growth. It is possible and really quite probable that he will mistake the other's views and make wrong use of the tools which his image puts into his hands. A man must be willing to be correct a part of the time. He will never be right all of the time. A constant self-examination is called for. A man must watch for danger signs.

The first of these danger signs would be " the enjoyment of cynicism." When too much contentment or too much shrugging of the shoulders is evident in life, there is danger of comfort. Health-giving tension has been relaxed. On the other hand, there is a depression that can overcome the man who has set his goal on perfection and is not able to find peace anywhere. Both of these are to be avoided. There is freedom in the ministry if a man can be a professional without cynicism. If a man can look at the opportunity afforded by his office and grasp that opportunity with enthusiasm, he can be useful. If he can be free of inhibition when this is appropriate, and restrict his behavior for the good of others, if he is willing to look at his own motivation honestly and not be depressed when he comes off less than perfect, then he has a chance for both usefulness and freedom in his work. Besides this, if he will take the trouble to cultivate a few Jewish friends, he can be a thorough human being.

Epilogue

The ministry is a profession in which the primary thrust of responsibility is toward the health of the visible church. The church is fallible and secular but the professional in its service is committed to faith in the valid mission of that secular body of believers.

All the professions carry with them a set of expectations in the minds of the people who are served by the professional. These expectations can be used for positive good, or, if ignored, they can be perverted to serve as the basis for rationalization or unhealthy dependence on the part of others. It is an important part of professional responsibility to see that these expectations are properly used.

The minister has three choices when he faces the fact that he carries this residue of expectation. He can attempt to eliminate it, he can accept it as whole truth, or he can be professionally responsible and use the expectations of others in creative ways.

I have attempted, in this volume, to set down what seem to be some of the creative ways in which a man can make use of the opportunities available to him through the expectations of others. There has been an appeal for objectivity, humility, a sense of reality, and professional responsibility. Most important of all, a minister must have a faith in the potential of resurrection and a faith that he understands and can apply to real life situations. His faith must be translatable.

The minister has a right to his own humanity. More than this, he has a responsibility to be human. It is the contention of this book that he can be human and a professional at the same time if he will accept the limitations of his profession honestly.

Notes

1. Samuel W. Blizzard, "The Parish Minister's Self-image of His Master Role," in Wayne E. Oates, ed., *The Minister's Own Mental Health* (Channel Press, 1961), pp. 113–114.

2. Robert McAfee Brown, *The Significance of the Church* (The Westminster Press, 1956), p. 17.

3. John Updike, *Rabbit, Run* (Crest Books, Fawcett Publications, Inc., 1964), pp. 142–143.

4. Fritz Kunkel, *In Search of Maturity* (Charles Scribner's Sons, 1955), pp. 262 ff.

5. James Knight, *A Psychiatrist Looks at Religion and Health* (Abingdon Press, 1964), pp. 180 ff.

6. Edmund Bergler, *Counterfeit-Sex: Homosexuality, Impotence, Frigidity* (Grove Press, Inc., 1961).

7. Editor, "Dangerous Mission," *The Christian Century*, Vol. LXXXIII, No. 20 (May 18, 1966).

8. Albert Camus, *Resistance, Rebellion, and Death* (Alfred A. Knopf, Inc., 1961), p. 71.

9. Wesner Fallaw, *Church Education for Tomorrow* (The Westminster Press, 1960), pp. 72–73.

10. Willard Waller, *Sociology of Teaching* (Science Editions, John Wiley & Sons, Inc., 1961), pp. 375–409. Copyright 1932 by John Wiley & Sons, Inc.